Living with
Uncertainty
and Still Enjoying
LIFE

---

*A Family Survival Guide
for Lives Interrupted by a Crisis*

Never be afraid to trust an unknown future to
a known God.
—Corrie Ten Boom

Karen Kay Dunn, M.A.

WESTBOW
PRESS®
A DIVISION OF THOMAS NELSON
& ZONDERVAN

All Scripture quotations are taken from the New Revised Standard Version of the Bible (NRSV). Copyright 1989, by the Division of Christian Education of the National Council of the Churches of Christ in the United States of America. Used by permission. All rights reserved.

Author Credits: Karen Kay Dunn—*Who's Who in Healthcare and Medicine, Who's Who in America, Who's Who in the World.*

WestBow Press books may be ordered through booksellers or by contacting:

WestBow Press
A Division of Thomas Nelson & Zondervan
1663 Liberty Drive
Bloomington, IN 47403
www.westbowpress.com
1 (866) 928-1240

ISBN: 978-1-5127-7720-8 (sc)
ISBN: 978-1-5127-7721-5 (hc)
ISBN: 978-1-5127-7719-2 (e)

Library of Congress Control Number: 2017903262

Print information available on the last page.

WestBow Press rev. date: 04/17/2017

CONTENTS

DEDICATION

This book is dedicated to my husband, children and grandchildren.

We are all learning to live with uncertainty while keeping joy and peace in our lives.

My husband and children (Stan Dunn, Michelle Trippe, and Stan Dunn II) have been my cheerleaders and devoted countless hours in helping me write and edit *Living with Uncertainty and Still Enjoying Life*. This book would probably never have existed without their extremely valuable input.

PREFACE

Your world has just stopped in its tracks. I know mine did! You've been bombarded with devastating words. Cancer, Alzheimer's disease, Parkinson's disease, catastrophic losses, debilitating injury, death, divorce, suicide, financial ruin, and terminal illness are among the most alarming words in the human language. Words that explode in your ears as they indicate that you and your family are now on a journey of living with uncertainty, clouding your future and troubling your soul. They will—if you let them—topple you in the midst of your crisis. An earthquake has struck at your very foundation, and recovering from it will be no easy task.

Having spent the better part of my career counseling individuals battling various forms of trauma, I was only somewhat prepared when my dermatologist used the word "cancer" to describe a spot on my leg. I hoped, if it was malignant, it would be nothing worse than an easily cured basal cell carcinoma. I certainly hoped it would not be a melanoma—otherwise known as "the deadly skin cancer." My internist did a biopsy and, after several tense days, I was informed that the local labs were unable to give a definite diagnosis so they sent the biopsy to Mayo Clinic. The inconclusive diagnoses briefly provided hope that the troubling spot on my leg might not be malignant. I hoped that this was a short nightmare from which I would soon awake.

In the meantime, I was referred to an oncological dermatologist for the excision of the growth. He took one look at it and said I should prepare for it being a melanoma. Having taught about melanomas at the University of Colorado Medical School after doing his fellowship at Harvard Medical School, I knew he was well qualified to make such a statement. My hope for a return to life as it had been faded as he surgically removed the black spot and sent it to the lab. The results were expected to take several days. When I received a call from him early the next morning, I had a strong suspicion that it was bad news.

My worst fears were confirmed when I was informed it was indeed melanoma and that it had the three most troubling elements in it. They found evidence of mitosis, ulceration, and growth deep into the skin with a Breslow's thickness exceeding 1mm. All of these elements meant that my malignant cells were creating new cancer cells and were sending them into other areas of my body. I knew the thinner the malignancy, the better the chance for a cure. Mine was not thin. Mine was classified as an *invasive* melanoma! This diagnosis was later confirmed by Mayo Clinic and MD Anderson Cancer Center, so I had little avenue left for denial. I was at Stage II of four stages of advancing cancer. This was day one of my experience (and my family's experience) in living with uncertainty. What would our future look like?

With melanoma, uncertainty is destined to become a fact of life. You are not "cured" when you have a diagnosis of advanced metastatic melanoma. You may go into remission, but it can, and usually does, return after the remission.

It is a challenge not to panic or give up hope when your joy over going into remission becomes disrupted by another tumor. There is nothing like living in a state of perpetual uncertainty to force you to forget the small stuff and just live life. When tremors knock the china from the cabinet, you can either be upset at the mess it left behind or be grateful for the things that remain.

Not to let myself be defeated and depressed by my devastating diagnosis, I went into a problem solving mode which generated hope. Knowing how very serious my melanoma was from the beginning, I had chosen MD Anderson Cancer Center in Houston, Texas for my treatment. I knew that they were not only a world-class cancer center, but also a world-renowned research center who were creating out of the box treatments and were achieving improving survival rates. I knew I needed a medical facility which was constantly breaking paradigms in their innovative but scientifically sound treatment approaches. The simple act of choosing MD Anderson Cancer Center injected me with a much needed dose of hope.

When you are in a fight with cancer, hope can be a tenuous and fleeting thing. Not long after I started treatment, the melanoma became very aggressive, with seven new melanomas popping up on my leg in one day—a local metastasis in the medical jargon. In plain English, it was spreading through my leg. This is, of course, not what you want to hear: your malignancy is aggressively spreading!

Five months later, there gradually emerged several more melanomas in that leg and evidence that the malignancy had moved into my lymph system. Thirty five lymph nodes were removed, twenty one of which were diseased with melanoma! I was now advanced to stage three cancer, and the highest category, Stage IIIC. My new diagnosis became advanced metastatic malignant melanoma, a diagnosis that carried with it a poor prognosis for a cure and a shortened life span spelled out in months instead of years.

I was fortunate to have a truly amazing and encouraging surgeon at MD Anderson Cancer Center assigned to my case, Dr. Merrick Ross. Because of his excellence and the expertise of his team, as well as many prayers from others for my healing, the cancer was slowed down against all odds. I know it was God who gave me a break after over two years of suffering. That remission lasted a wonderful two and a half years!

Just recently, this respite was disrupted by a routine scan which indicated that the melanoma had spread to my small intestine. A biopsy confirmed that diagnosis. I had progressed to the dreaded Stage IV.

I am living with uncertainty regarding my future and will be for the remainder of my time on this earth. I have learned that life can be full of joy and new adventures even when your outlook is hazy. I want to share with you the insights that have been gained by a diverse group of individuals who have succeeded at maintaining peace and joy in spite of difficult life circumstances.

Living with uncertainty and still finding ways to enjoy life is an attainable goal. Most of us would not volunteer for a difficult life passage, but that does not stop a life crisis from suddenly erupting. Some calamity happens from time to time in every life.

Who would invite a serious or potentially terminal disease, loss of a job, financial crisis, estrangement from close friends or family members, divorce, death of a loved one, loss of physical capacity, memory loss, or any other tragedy into their life? These appear without invitation.

When moving through a significant life crisis, it is easy for you and your loved ones to feel like you are flying through a thick fog while experiencing vertigo, not knowing which way is up and which way is down. In such confusion, pilots most ignore their basic senses and trust their instruments to have any hope of a safe landing.

Everything in our world may feel like it is turned upside down! Many things that seemed really important may suddenly have turned out to not be so important after all! In learning to live with uncertainty, it is important that we refocus ourselves on making a safe landing through life enhancing decisions, rather than giving up and letting ourselves experience a crash.

You are likely reading this book because you are going through a difficult journey with no assurances as to what the outcome will be. You could feel like you are driving on an icy mountain road with a steep drop-off at the edge. You may be uncertain about whether you can stay on the path, as well as concerned about what you will encounter around the bend. Depending upon your personality and past experience, you could feel terrified when you unexpectedly find yourself on a challenging road of no return.

Another option is that you could be one who immediately sees it as a challenge while you slip into conquering mode. You would probably hope that this treacherous road will lead to a great reward when you have finished the journey. A few of you might even consider this road to be a reward in itself. It is all a matter of perspective when we find ourselves suddenly living with uncertain outcomes.

> When written in Chinese, the word 'crisis' is composed of two characters—one represents danger, and the other represents opportunity.
> —John F Kennedy

If you are not presently going through a life crisis, you may be reading this because someone you love is in a tough situation and struggling to find a way to adjust to unsettling uncertainty. Unpleasant circumstances in our lives, which bring about new realities, require that we find effective tools to stop them from overwhelming us. This book will familiarize you with some useful tools to regain peace and joy in your life (or help another person) despite enduring, uninvited life circumstances. You must first regain your peace and joy before you can become a source of peace and joy to others. This is true for those going through uncertain life events, as well as for those standing beside them.

Have you ever closely examined snowflakes? They come in various designs, sizes, and shapes. What causes them to usually be so different? Snowflake development is influenced by temperature and humidity, as well as the path taken on the journey to you.

What is true for snowflake development is true also for people. While we share many common traits based on our human nature, we are also unique in some special ways. This means that each person expresses their life crisis in both a predictable (based on their humanness) and an unpredictable (based on their individual uniqueness) way. The adverse or friendly conditions we pass through in our lifetime influence our design as a person and our somewhat predictable reactions to unpleasant circumstances.

Unlike the snowflake (which makes no decision on its journey) we do have some influence on both our path and outcome, despite the occasional circumstances that are out of our control. We have an extraordinary ability to control our outlook as we approach the sometimes chaotic events that disturb our day to day existence.

This book will focus on the positive, encouraging influence we can still have in our lives, even while battling extreme life crises, handicapping events, or serious diseases with uncertain outcomes.

A lesson to be learned in passing through a crisis is that dire circumstances do not always lead to the worst possible outcome. Time and experience can drastically assuage our original fears. During the past five years, my family and I have been living with uncertainty regarding my survival, but not letting it steal our joy! I know other patients who have survived with my diagnosis for over a decade. This is unusual but encouraging to me.

I am so glad that I chose not to waste my life and time by hanging out in a dark cloud of depression while cancer has been a part of my life. I may not have much choice in how my disease progresses, but I do get a choice in how I respond to it.

I am, by nature, a nurturing person. Because of this (and seeing the effect on family and friends of the uncertainty caused by my medical crisis), I wanted to nurture them. It turns out that this was a very good choice since I nurtured myself in the process. I made a decision early on that, despite my cancer and the ravaging effects of it and the treatments, I would continue to live my life to the fullest for whatever amount of time that I had left! I would not allow cancer to be the focus of my life! The same attitude was true of others revealed in this book who encountered a variety of other troubling life circumstances. *They decided not to let their crisis take away their joy or peace.* They focused on the remainder of their lives as a gift, instead of focusing on their particular troubles as a curse.

There are two important aspects to conquering a life crisis. One is attempting to move as quickly as possible, away from focusing on it, to a new focus on identifying and bravely approaching possible solutions. Following this is the process of adapting to the unpleasant situation itself, learning how to live with it day to day. *Regardless of what the life crisis was, the people discussed in this book have learned to promptly start searching for a problem solving technique that gives them the best chance of making it through with the least possible damage.*

The second equally important aspect is conquering and defeating the detrimental emotional effects that the crisis can have on the affected person and their loved ones. *Attitude is an important factor in the healing process, after encountering significant uncertainties in life.*

Over time, I came to understand that when one member of a family has cancer, all members (figuratively speaking) have cancer. To put this another way, *when one member of a family is going through a critical passage in their life, the whole family connected with them is going through that critical passage with them in some form. The same is true of close friends and other loved ones.* They are also affected by your crisis and how you respond to it.

One of the things we will explore is how others made it through foreboding periods in their lives while maintaining their joy. We will look at their method of experiencing the best quality of life under their circumstances. You will hear stories of brave people passing through life traumas, yet somehow finding a way to live a full and impactful life during their otherwise unpleasant life circumstances.

Throughout my career as a Mental Health Therapist, I have found that relationships with loved ones and with God have a highly effective transformative effect on healing from struggles with trauma. The holistic effect of treating not only emotions, but relationships and spiritual connectedness as well, promote healing from struggles with trauma. I know it did for me! Individuals that fail to seek out and nurture their relationships with loved ones and with God are missing out on the most powerful way to survive their crisis with their sanity intact.

Most people prefer to go through life without any troubling crises involving uncertain outcomes. We want predictable, happy ever after lives. I know that would be my preference. However, the reality is that our lives are more complicated than that. Our lives occasionally are interspersed with unpleasant experiences. Sometimes, it is not possible to accurately predict when these will come or what the outcome will be. Learning to live with uncertainty and not letting it steal our joy or overall satisfaction with life is a noble goal. With a combination of the right processes and a lot of prayer, it is obtainable.

My approach in this book is to look at life's uncertainties from the affected person's standpoint. The goal is to provide encouragement as well as a process that helps conquer fear and improve quality of life while walking through a challenging journey. Even beyond that, it is possible to keep some joy and happiness through any difficult journey.

How can that be? There will be moments of sadness in this journey. There are techniques and mindsets which have been proven to help individuals maintain a positive outlook in their lives, even through very dark and disturbing crises. The intent here is to effectively describe a wide range of those approaches, so that you can find hope even in the midst of your uncertainty.

> God is our refuge and strength,
> a very present help in trouble.
> —Psalm 46:1

> And let the peace of Christ rule in your hearts.
> —Colossians 3:15a

> I know that there is nothing better for them than to be
> happy and enjoy themselves as long as they live.
> —Ecclesiastes 3:12a

CHAPTER 1

When Life Takes a Detour: Now What Do I Do?

Life is 10% what happens to you and 90% how you react to it.
—Charles Swindoll, *The Grace Awakening*

Don't cling to a mistake just because you spent a lot of time making it.
—Unknown

Detour signs have a tendency to frustrate me. I know the path I am on, but that path is suddenly not passable and I am forced on an unfamiliar road. Detours can make us feel uncertain whether we will be able to find our way back to the destination. Sometimes, the detour is not well marked and our intuition can lead us astray. We end up getting lost as our uninformed decisions jumble our sense of direction.

We encounter emotional detours when we find ourselves face-to-face with crises in our lives. They change the rules and block the direction we were traveling in. Uncertainty sets in. This leaves us wondering if our life will ever be the same again.

Have you experienced an excruciating uncertainty about how a life crisis will end? How many times in the past did you fear the worst-case scenario would come about? How many times did it actually occur? If you are like most people, the worst-case scenario never occurred. Think about all the time and energy we waste pondering a worst-case scenario …

If you focus on what you left behind, you will never see what lies ahead! Strain to look ahead instead of being fixed on an unpleasant time in your past or your present.

Remember that tomorrow is a blank page in the journal of your life. Write a great page! You are the author of that story. You get to choose what you write on the pages ahead of you.

Failing Forward

John C Maxwell wrote an interesting book called *Failing Forward*. The concept of failing forward is overcoming your failures by using the lessons you learned from a failure to improve your future performance.

When our children were younger, they occasionally found themselves experiencing challenging situations in which they felt devastated by their personal failures. Following those times, my husband wisely counseled them to "fail forward." He was helping them avoid staying stuck in the failure, and encouraging them to move forward armed with the knowledge gained by that experience, in order to build a bright future for themselves.

Using that life illustration, an acronym for the word *fail* could be FAIL: finding another insightful lesson. Our crises are learning experiences when we bring forward the positive lessons to minimize future failures.

An important rule to follow when you find yourself in a life crisis is—do not go to the end of your life in your mind, especially if your imagination is coming up with a negative end. The end is not yet here.

You can deal with whatever you actually have to deal with when that time comes. Even if you have been told that your condition is terminal, if you are reading this, you still have time left. Make that time as meaningful as possible. You may have much more time than you think you do.

My friend Tom had an inoperable brain tumor and was told he had four to six months to live. Against all odds, he lived seven years after that. My prognosis was that I only had months to live, and here I am pressing on into my sixth year.

Our Crisis Does not Define Us

Remember that our crisis does not define us. Optimistically assume that you have the strength and wisdom to turn an unpleasant crisis into a positive outcome. Optimism that is still in touch with reality serves us well when navigating a crisis. We can accomplish amazing things as we emerge from a life crisis as long as we stubbornly refuse to let it engulf and define us.

A butterfly is a good example of a creature that moves from darkness into light. The butterfly starts its life as a caterpillar, crawling its way through life. Then, in a crisis like situation, the caterpillar weaves an outer covering that brings it into darkness. It is this environment which allows the butterfly to transform itself from a caterpillar—from a slinking, crawling creature—into a flying wonder of beauty.

Let your crisis situation stimulate you to embark on a beautiful transformation in your life. You may feel like you are crawling now, but you can emerge soaring if you focus on constructing a hopeful future.

The Calm After the Storm

Remember that there is calm after the storm. Ultimately, perfect calm comes after we pass from this life into the eternal one. The good news is that we don't have to wait until the end to experience a spiritual and emotional calm—it is available in the midst of a storm.

Sometimes you can't control the things that happen to you, but you can always have some control over how you react to them.

> Be strong and courageous; do not be frightened or dismayed, for the LORD your God is with you wherever you go.
> —Joshua 1:9

Life is filled with unexpected turns and unforeseen problems. Sometimes these become the beginning of a life crisis. Other times, they are brief and dissipate on their own. One part of being human is the capacity to rise above our current circumstances. Periods of instability in our lives enable us to cultivate coping mechanisms for future use.

What life crisis are you facing? Is it health related? Is it the loss of relationship with a loved one due to estrangement, divorce, death, Alzheimer's, accident, or other cause? Does it involve financial crisis due to the loss of a job, stock market crash, or overspending?

It doesn't matter what the life crisis is. What matters is how you approach it. *How you approach the crisis can result in a worsening of the situation, or it can limit it from stealing more than it already has.*

Let's start by analyzing human emotions in responding to unpleasant situations, and then we will go on in subsequent chapters to see how we can still have a life—with joy and peace in it—in spite of the chaos.

Life is interesting, isn't it? One moment you are cruising along, loving the view, and the next moment you find yourself in the midst of a storm.

You may feel like you have lost the oars and your canoe (the crisis) is now determining your course. Worse yet, the erratic movement of the canoe within the storm leaves you fearful that you may not be able to remain upright, resulting in a struggle for survival.

A calm and serene life turns into an adventure that you never asked for or wanted. Waves come in life, and it is better to have a surfboard handy than to pretend there will be no waves. Though your serenity may be temporarily taken away, you can regain joy once you learn how to ride the waves.

What Nature Teaches Us

In many ways, nature mimics our life journey. Let's look at trees and seasons as an example of this. Just as trees go through seasonal changes, so do we experience transformations resulting from our passages in life. There are times when life is pleasant. It is like being in the springtime of our lives. We are thriving, growing, and productive during those periods. Trees put on fresh new leaves during the spring. Flowers bloom, young life abounds, and nature captivates us by newfound beauty. All is well and life is beautiful. Our correlation to nature's renewal time is when we are passing through a pleasant life season, bringing new zest and vigor into our lives.

> How precious is your steadfast love, O God!
> All people may take refuge in the shadow of your wings.
> —Psalm 36:7

When the heat of summer feels unbearable, we can remain under trees and enjoy the relief their shade gives on warm, sunny days. Relationships thrive and romance blooms. It is like taking refuge in the shadow of loving wings. Under the shadow of God's wings is a great place to rest when life is feeling unbearable.

> The LORD God appointed a bush, and made it come up over Jonah, to give shade over his head, to save him from his discomfort; so Jonah was very happy about the bush.
> —Jonah 4:6

Figuratively speaking, although the heat of summer can become uncomfortable at times, the summer of our lives produces rest and nourishment for us. It is a fulfilling and mature time in our lives. It makes us strong so we can face the storms that come as we wander through life.

The true color of nature is unlocked in autumn. High mountain peaks gain white caps, while a canopy of color invades the forests. Our neighbor's little girl referred to the fall beauty in our neighborhood as "the rainbow forest," which it was. It was lovelier than the eye could take in all at once.

Our true color often comes out when we are nearing the end of autumn and have the winter of our lives approaching. The beauty we choose to emit remains in our control, even on the precipice of our crisis. We can emit vibrant and exciting colors—a feast for the eyes and heart—if we decide to do so, despite the heavy load of our personal crisis.

 Next comes winter with harsh cold and storms that strip the leaves from the trees. You could correlate that to the crisis periods in our lives. The good news for the trees is that this seasonal pattern is only temporary, so the tree is not permanently stuck in winter.

We benefit when we remind ourselves that the tree, or our crisis of uncertainty, doesn't stay in the bare state of winter forever. Winter is followed by spring. Eventually, the tree grows leaves again. In the cycle of our lives—when we find ourselves in nature's correlate of winter—remember, if we are patient, better times are likely ahead of us. As Joyce Meyer said, "When we worry about tomorrow, we waste today."

This is the good news for us. We may feel during and after a crisis that our happy lives have been stripped away from us forever. We may feel bare and unprotected from the storms. Remember that our lives can be every bit as cyclical as nature. We have periods in our lives that are fresh and new, productive and mature, yet these are sometimes interrupted by unpleasant circumstances. Given time, life crises abate. Whether on earth or in eternity, we eventually will resume the process of continuing to grow and thrive.

We will adjust to difficult situations and go on with our lives unless we choose to stay stuck in the "poor me" pit of depression. Depression is both physically and emotionally harmful to the body when it is allowed to persist over time. We cannot avoid brief periods which are so unsettling that we may become temporarily depressed, but it is a choice whether we allow those episodes of depression to go on for longer periods of time. We can instead dispense with depression and find enjoyment in the remainder of our lives.

If you let yourself, you may end up dwelling in the pit of depression for years. What a sad loss of irretrievable time when we allow that to happen!

> I will put off my sad countenance and be of good cheer.
> —Job 9:27b

> Anxiety weighs down the human heart,
> but a good word cheers it up.
> —Proverbs 12:25

A Crisis is Like an Erupting Volcano

As a volcano is erupting, people in the vicinity of the volcano are thrust into a survival mode which requires relatively quick planning and action to minimize their losses. Among the first decisions people need to make is, "What do I need to do to survive this? Where is a safe place that I can go to protect myself from being destroyed? I can replace my house, but I cannot replace me. What do I need to do next?"

Quick action is needed to help people protect themselves from being destroyed by the erupting volcano. In the developed world, we are surrounded by governmental agencies who plan for and enact rescue plans. They have been trained for this very situation and can lead you to safety, if you will listen and obey. There is safe ground, but sometimes we need others to assist us in finding it.

A crisis in our life is very much like the eruption of a volcano or a rapidly spreading wildfire. It happens very quickly and often without warning. In some cases (as in the impending death of a loved one) we do have some advance warning, while in other cases we do not. Seismologists who measure the earth's activity around a volcano will generally have advance notice of the impending danger. They can measure the series of tremors that precede the lava flow. They are the ones who warn of the danger.

We may encounter seismic tremors which point to the possibility that a crisis is looming. This could be produced by a multitude of experiences: a serious illness; forgetfulness becoming routine; a financial downturn resulting in a round of furloughs; your spouse growing distant from you; you/your child/your friend becoming depressed, etc. However, there are some times—like in a serious accident—that the crisis comes with no forewarning.

Sometimes, we are quickly able to come up with a plan to protect ourselves in the midst of an eruptive crisis. Occasionally, we follow that plan. Other times, like in an eruption, we need to seek out the experts who have been trained to equip people to survive. Help is available, if only we seek it out.

What do erupting volcanos have to do with crisis management? During the eruptive phase of a volcano, people are so intent on surviving that they seek only what they need to do to survive the next moment. But what happens after they are safely away from the crisis, and are now encountering the after effects of the destruction?

Hope After the Eruption

This is where hope comes in. When you are in the midst of unfortunate circumstances, it is natural to myopically focus on them and ignore the future possibilities that hope can unlock. Though a river of lava in your living room is devastating, hope is ready to help you rebuild.

Something will continue to grow after an eruption in life's flow... and it will probably be YOU!

When a volcano erupts, the flowing lava wipes out everything in its path. It may be initially successful in that venture—but, in the long run, new life breaks out through the formerly destructive flow. For a season, it looks like the destruction is so complete that life will never look the same again. Over time, however, the red hot lava cools down and creates a fertile ground for new growth.

Even though life does not look exactly the same after a volcanic eruption, it can eventually inspire wonder—different but still delightful. Sometimes, it can look much more beautiful after the eruption than it did before. The intensely beautiful Hawaiian Islands (among others) would never have existed, save for an endless supply of volcanic eruptions.

Our dim view of our future after our encounter with uncertainty may feel like the path of destruction that follows a river of lava. Remember, despite the damage you are currently experiencing, rebuilding takes place only when we are courageous enough to start that process. Temporary desolation can become a work of beauty given some time.

All you have to do to witness this metamorphosis is to visit Hawaii or any of the chain of islands created by devastating eruptions but are now tropical islands of immense beauty: places where people flock for peace, rest, and recreation. Like lush greenery pressing through the charcoal lava fields, you can produce incredible beauty after your experience with uncertainty regarding your future is over.

One thing we know for sure, *we will have periods of suffering in this world, but we also need to be aware that we are not in this alone.* We have someone to comfort us in our suffering. Many of us have family and friends and medical personnel encouraging us through the crisis. Even when we do not feel like anyone else knows how to comfort us in this storm, we can look to heaven for support and comfort when it is needed.

Our first reaction to a crisis is often disbelief, denial, shock. Can this really be happening to me? The sooner we turn in prayer for wisdom and comfort—the sooner we realize that we are not alone—the faster a cathartic relief will begin to settle in. Family and friends are likely weeping with us over the distress we feel. Knowing God is right there with us can give us the peace that passes understanding as we journey through this suffering episode.

> So we do not lose heart. Even though our outer nature is wasting away, our inner nature is being renewed day by day. For this slight momentary affliction is preparing us for an eternal weight of glory beyond all measure,

because we look not at what can be seen but at what cannot be seen; for what can be seen is temporary, but what cannot be seen is eternal.
—2Corinthians 4:16–18

It is worth repeating here, the one thing certain in this life is that we will encounter uncertainty and unpleasant circumstances which will overwhelm us from time to time. We still have a choice when this happens. We may allow this to cripple us and steal our joy, or choose to overcome the harmful effects by determining to have the fullest life possible in the midst of our trials.

Become a Problem Solver

There are some effective approaches for successfully adjusting to (or conquering) a life crisis. The first step is to search for possible solutions to solve the crisis. *People who easily become overwhelmed when faced with a significant uncertainty in their lives are often those who keep their focus fixed on the problem. Focusing on the problem can be a cause of hopelessness. Focusing on a possible solution results in hopefulness.*

Hopelessness feels like being engulfed in darkness. There are ways out of the darkness of any situation that will lead you into the light of hopefulness again. We will be discussing some of them in this book.

> Courage doesn't always roar. Sometimes courage is the quiet voice at the end of the day, saying, 'I will try again tomorrow.'
> —Mary Anne Radmacher, *Courage Doesn't Always Roar*

> The past will be our future until we have the courage to create a new one.
> —Erwin McManus, Global Leadership Summit

The only way you can get rid of darkness is to turn on the light. Better than this, the person who decides not to sit in darkness can simply open the blinds to let the sun shine in. Even if the sunlight is not enough to totally emerge the room in color, it will at least chase the worst of the gray away. We choose searching for the source of light rather than decompensation. The Light of the World drives out our darkness.

Decompensation is the process of allowing deterioration to take place in you, which thrusts you into deep darkness. In psychological terms, decompensation is losing your ability to maintain normal psychological defenses, resulting in going deeper into depression, anxiety, or delusional fears. The good news is that you do not need to make the choice to descend into the madness that this has to offer. There is a light switch of hopefulness nearby. Go searching for it until you find it. Flee the darkness in search of the light.

Regardless of what the life crisis is, quickly start searching for a problem solving technique which gives the best chance of making it through with as little collateral damage as possible. If it is a life-threatening medical problem, find excellent doctors to guide you then attempt to bravely approach the treatments in order to physically conquer and defeat the health problem. If a financial problem, consult with financial experts (or a friend who is very good at managing their own finances). If loss of a relationship due to death, estrangement, or dementia, look for and join a support group to help you adjust. If loss of a job, network to find a new job. In short, identify the problem and then brainstorm solutions and begin to implement the best solutions until one works! Stop allowing fear to control you.

Overcoming Fear

> Do not fear, for I am with you,
> do not be afraid, for I am your God;
> I will strengthen you, I will help you,
> I will uphold you with my victorious right hand.
> —Isaiah 41:10

O Most High, when I am afraid,
I put my trust in you.
—Psalm 56:2b–3

Courage is not the absence of fear ...
Courage is the willingness to act in spite of my fear.
—Michael Hyatt, *Platform: Get Noticed in a Noisy World*

Who you are in the space when you can't see in front
of you is where courage is born ... I want to be in the
arena ... to be brave with my life.
—Dr. Brene Brown, *Rising Strong*

Courage isn't having the strength to go on ... it is going
on when you don't have strength.
—unknown

Sometimes fear enters into the crisis situation instead of courage. It would do you well to remember that *fear is something you create in your mind*. Knowing that you create those thoughts in your head allows you to understand *if you can create them, you can also conquer and dispel them from your mind*. Fear freezes you and discourages you from trying to muster up the courage you need to effectively endure a crisis. Fear is the lie that escape is the only alternative to this situation.

The truth is that escape is most often a counterproductive aggravation of your crisis. Danger may exist and be very real, but fear is a fabrication of letting your mind go into negative spaces. Even the Bible repeatedly says, "Do not fear!" Don't make the choice to allow fear to take up residence in your mind. Instead, focus on potential solutions that will serve as an antidote to fear.

Do. Not. Live. In. Fear.
—Greg Coplen

In behavioral psychology, we talk about thought stopping and thought substitution. These are very effective techniques for dealing with fear. Bob Newhart has a comedy episode on YouTube that is called, "Stop It!" I would encourage you to take a moment to see that skit. It is an example of this technique. We will more fully discuss this concept later in this book.

Sometimes, we may be unable to find a good solution to the crisis. We may simply need the courage to walk through the uncertainty when solutions are limited. It always helps to walk through these uncertainties with someone who loves you.

> The LORD is near to the brokenhearted.
> —Psalm 34:18

Another situation involves a crisis that cannot be changed by you. Examples of this could be a debilitating health problem; economic instability caused by the society you live in; your spouse divorcing you and unwilling to reconcile; a child running away from home; the death of a loved one; a good friend rejecting you, etc.

You may not be able to solve the problem, but you can stop the problem from destroying your peace and joy. *Although the crisis is a part of your life, choose not to let it define your life. We remove the adverse power of our crisis by stubbornly refusing to let it become our absolute singular focus.*

A Time to Grieve and a Time to Rest

The unfortunate circumstances you are passing through may have caused grieving and tears. It is normal and even advisable to release your emotions in beneficial ways, but *everyone needs to build periods of rest into their time of grieving.*

Spend time doing what is relaxing to you to give yourself breaks. Many people find rest in going for nature walks, quiet times reading the Bible and other books, listening to music, and playing games with friends—especially where laughter is involved. Laughter may not solve the crisis, but it can give needed breaks.

Emotional instability makes a bad situation worse. Emotional stability will make the crisis impotent from being able to gain excessive control of your life. A key to successfully making it through the crisis period is to realize that your intense pain will pass with time. Hopefully, techniques described in this book will help give you the courage and determination to stop this situation from taking away from you any more than its due share.

The Healing Power of Relationships

The healing power of relationships cannot be overstated. Journeys into uncertainty might lead you to some wonderful people. Decide to enjoy being around the ones you love and who love you, and help them enjoy being around you as you walk through this time of uncertainty together. You don't have to face this alone. When you most need to receive encouragement from others, encourage someone else. After doing so, you may find you receive more inspiration that you can then apply to your own life. You lift yourself up when you take the time to lift others up. Nurture the wonderful people in your life as they are reaching out to you.

Bless people by asking for the help that you need. Don't overwhelm them by expecting them to devote all their time and effort to helping you adjust to your new uncertainties in life. On the other hand, don't think that you need to go through this passage alone. Remember that God is always available to give you compassion and wise counsel. Friends, family members, doctors, counselors, pastors, and other professionals have very wise counsel and encouragement to give if you will just seek it from them.

Just as people can be our best asset while we are journeying through uncertain times, some can also increase our pain when we are exhausted from the struggle. Either through their own failings or as a result of their own life struggles, we may perceive that they are being unkind to us instead of giving us the emotional support that we need. When we are worried, afraid, or stressed, we have a tendency to become overly sensitive. We compound the issue if we allow ourselves to misinterpret a statement or an attitude of another person, and let it destroy our peace.

Seeking Advice from Others

Seek needed advice from others. Business leaders do not make the best decisions in isolation. A decision making process that requires only a single individual's input is only effective for very simple problems. Anything remotely complex is going to be most effectively solved by a social interaction.

Great managers know that if they want to come up with incredible solutions, the Delphi method is a superior approach. In the Delphi method, the manager gathers together knowledgable people in the issue at hand. The discussions that result produce something noteworthy. In talking to and listening to each other, synergism takes place where the best solution becomes evident as a result of their discussion. Solutions arrived through synergism are uniformly superior to those proposed by one person independently of others.

Use this knowledge to your advantage. Utilize the people and resources available to you while making decisions as to how to approach your crisis situation to achieve the superior result. Seek the wise counsel of experts in the type of a crisis you are facing. Don't choose to be a loner. Ultimately, after you receive feedback from these people, the decision as to how to proceed is still yours to make, but it will help you to realize better options in making your decision.

Facing Hard Realities

I lived the first four years following my diagnosis in the perpetual reality that my lifespan might be limited to a handful of months. Though my life continued to be extended by the grace of God and the expertise of doctors, the possibility of a sharp turn to an earlier grave was continually before me. I immediately went into a mode of trying to put my affairs in order in case my life was going to quickly end.

I went Christmas shopping early and wrapped the presents so each of my loved ones would still receive a loving gift from me, even if I were not there to give it. I made a firm decision for myself that, despite this disease, I would not let it steal my peace.

An interesting thing occurred in my life. My focus moved off of me and instead it moved onto the family and friends I might be leaving behind. I wanted this transition on them to be as uncomplicated as possible. I wanted to protect them from fear and anxiety caused by my disease and of the possibility that I would not be with them much longer. I did not want my disease to be the focus of their lives, just as I did not want it to be the focus of mine. It was unquestionably a part of my life now, but I could choose whether to allow it center stage, or to send it to the periphery. I deliberately chose a perspective that cancer was simply part of my life, not the focus of it. I wanted all of us to enjoy our lives, our relationships with each other, and continue to have as much of a life together as we could.

That was a huge goal! I assumed all the way through the process of the diagnoses, the treatments, the recuperation periods, even the hospitalizations, that I had set an achievable goal. I also knew my role would be crucial in the achievement of that goal. If this was my goal, I would need to be the one who kept my focus on making sure that I did all in my power to achieve that goal.

I was encouraged by knowing that this goal was achievable, with God's help. I started this journey by asking him to give me the courage, joy, endurance, peace, and wisdom I needed to guide myself and my loved ones into an emotionally healthy coping approach. I asked him to lead my medical team in wise decisions for my treatment. I learned that God is faithful to help you when you ask for help.

> My flesh and my heart may fail,
> but God is the strength of my heart and my portion forever.
> —Psalm 73:26

> Return to me, says the LORD of hosts, and I will return
> to you, says the LORD of hosts.
> —Zechariah 1:3

One thing that was very helpful to me was the knowledge that I knew how my story ended. I didn't know where, when, or how my story on earth would end, but I knew what my eternal life will be like. I had something immeasurably better than a fairytale ending to look forward to.

An eternal perspective helped me to not take the temporary life crisis I was in so seriously. *It was temporary.* My permanent life would be void of life crises, void of disease, and void of pain and loss! It would be an eternal embrace in love and contentment. As much as I was not ready to die (and I was *really* not ready to die), I had comfort in my eternal hope that gave me great peace during these otherwise chaotic years.

Stages of Adjusting to the Crisis

Elizabeth Kubler Ross, author of the book *On Death and Dying*, culminated her years of research on terminal patients by discovering five stages of adjustment to the potential of impending death. Actually, I have found that these steps often exist in any great life crisis or loss!

Not everyone goes through all of these steps or goes through them in the order described. The steps of adjustment she wrote about were denial, bargaining, depression, anger, and adjustment.

Denial Can be Our Friend

She identified the first step as being the emotional state of *denial*. (This is really not happening to me. It is just a bad dream I will awake from! I won't believe it has happened in my life! I don't believe the doctor—he/she must have misdiagnosed me or my loved one. The officer has a mistaken identity—my loved one was not killed. I won't accept that we are getting divorced—as far as I am concerned, we are still married and he/she will return to our marriage. The stock market crash will not leave me destitute since stocks will rise again as sharply as they dropped. He does not have dementia—everyone is forgetful from time to time.)

Denial, in the initial stages following the onset of the crisis, is the expression of the emotional shock that has invaded our life. It seems surreal and it takes time to absorb that the crisis is real. This is a normal reaction to an adverse situation. Most of us have experienced this temporary denial when encountering a significant life event that is disturbing to us.

Denial which persists over a longer period of time is more problematic and not a normal reaction. The bottom line on denial which persists over time is that people may be refusing to accept the facts of the situation, not knowing how they can accept such tragic news. They don't want to adapt to this tragedy in their life, so they simply pretend it never happened. The truth is that we *can* successfully adapt to significant crisis situations and the after effects they produce in our lives. The choice to not adjust almost always makes a bad situation worse.

The form of denial I encountered was questioning whether the diagnosis of melanoma was accurate. It was easy for me to go into denial when the initial diagnosis was inconclusive. It would have taken a great deal of self-deception to not believe the facts when both Mayo Clinic and MD Anderson Cancer Center independently examined the tissue and came up with the same diagnosis—invasive melanoma. I left denial behind me when I received that diagnosis. I accepted the truth of the situation, no matter how disconcerting it was.

I had a friend who was an amazing pastoral counselor. He and his wife had received the devastating news when they were expecting their fourth child that two of their children had a very serious genetic disease. Worse than that, they were told that the disease would likely take their lives before adulthood. One of those was their unborn baby. There was no available cure for the disease.

My friend described to us a very unique coping mechanism. He wanted to enjoy his children while they were with him and not stay focused on how short their lives could be. He said, "Denial has become my best friend."

That was how he chose to deal with this overwhelming situation in his life. Knowing the reality of the medical condition affecting his children, he chose not to dwell on it as he moved forward with his life and their lives. His vocation as a pastoral care counselor had him visiting individuals (sometimes terminal) who were walking through significant life crises.

I always admired how he could be dealing with the impending death of his children and still help others. My admiration was multiplied by the fact that he accomplished this difficult task with so much joy. His smile in the face of adversity was infectious and I am sure it had a great impact on those who he was helping overcome adversity. He didn't know it, but he was a good model for me as I was moving through this great uncertainty in my life. I decided to adopt his approach. He gave me an excellent example to follow while navigating through my life crisis.

This is an example of a beneficial use of denial. He was not really denying the truth of the diagnosis of his children. He accepted the reality of it. He merely chose to not let that reality occupy his thoughts while his children were still living. He hoped medical science would come up with a cure in time to save their lives. In the meantime, he did not want to waste away grieving while they were still alive! He did this so he could enjoy the remainder of their lives with them, not tainted by his impending loss of them.

He wasn't truly in denial because he accepted the truth of their disease. He made their life his focus instead of keeping his focus fixed on negative outcomes. He selfishly clung to his overall positive outlook on life, his sense of humor, and the peace that passes understanding that he asked for and received from God.

Let me point out again that it is not healthy nor beneficial to let yourself stay stuck in total denial, but it is good for you to be able to take breaks from the trauma when you are suffering. These moments of quasi denial can act as a fantastic coping mechanism. It also allows your body to get the rest it needs to facilitate your emotional or physical healing.

Another thing to remember and repeat here is—no matter how certain someone is about the final outcome of a situation—things can change. Take my friend who was told his children would not live into adulthood. Two of them are adults at this writing and the other approaching adulthood. Only God knows how your crisis will end, be resolved, or how you will grow from the crisis.

There was a lot of hype regarding the most recent blood moon rising. It is called a blood moon since it turns red during a total eclipse. Some people became concerned that it was a sign of the apocalypse—the end of the world as we know it. The fact that you are reading this indicates that the predictions of the world's demise were greatly exaggerated. The same could be true about the predictions you or others hold about the final outcome of the crisis that you are passing through.

During the first few years in my fight with advanced metastatic melanoma, the most reasonable prediction was that it was not likely that my life would last more than a few months longer. I am here now, many years later and counting forward.

It is possible to beat the odds of predicted and probable outcomes as we pass through our life crises. There are many stories where people survive when they were not expected to. Sometimes the survival is emotional and other times it is physical. In my case, it has been both. The cancer has come and gone multiple times now. I have been in remission but the cancer recently returned and I am once again fighting for my life. I refuse to be emotionally dead, no matter the continual nature of my life crisis. I will not allow the seriousness of my disease to rob me of the continual hope that I will survive to a grand old age.

I consider myself to be a realistic optimist. Those terms may seem incompatible when used together like that, but I do not think they are. The realistic part means that I don't deny the situation as it now stands, but the optimistic part means that I do know things can change and will not let anyone crush my hope. I prepare for the worst-case scenario, but do not accept that it is the only possible outcome.

Bargaining Doesn't Change the Crisis

The next step following denial is *bargaining*. (If only I had driven them to the game, they would not have had the accident. If I had eaten a healthier diet and didn't smoke or drink alcohol, I wouldn't have to deal with this heart attack, stroke, cancer, etc. If I hadn't invested all my savings in stocks, this wouldn't be happening to me. If I had been a more attentive parent and seen the signs of how depressed my child was, my child wouldn't have committed suicide.)

Bargaining comes after the person has broken through denial and accepts that this crisis really happened. They begin what we call *magical thinking*—pretending they could have done something to stop this crisis from occurring. This magical thinking gets stuck on trying to change the outcome of the crisis, when it is too late to do anything about it. Again, this is a normal early reaction to finding oneself in a crisis situation and is not problematic unless allowed to continue over a long period of time.

The form that bargaining took in my life crisis was going back two years in my mind when a friend asked me to see a doctor regarding that black spot on the calf of my leg. I forgot about it and let it grow on my leg for two years—let it grow until it became invasive. My bargaining was that if I had gone to a doctor earlier, the melanoma wouldn't have become invasive. Although this was likely true, I quickly left the bargaining stage because I recognized that I could not change my current situation by dwelling on my past choices. Emotionally beating myself up would not solve my current crisis, but would make it feel even worse than it was. I refused to do that.

The Power of Forgiveness

This brings me back to an earlier time in my life when I left the house later than I had planned to in order to get my young son to his soccer game. Without him being on time, the team would have had to forfeit the game (they would not have had enough players). Ten minutes after leaving home, I noticed the oil light came on in my car. I knew I should stop the car immediately to avoid engine damage, but decided to press through the final few miles to the game. There was a big problem with that decision, since my car stopped halfway to the soccer field.

In the end, my son made it to the game, but only because of the soccer mom (a friend of mine) that stopped when she noticed that we were broken down on the side of the road. My son went with her, and I sheepishly called my husband to bring our other (now only remaining) car to pick me up.

When I reached the soccer field, the story of what happened with my car preceded me through the parent who gave my son a ride. My friends came up to me, expressing their sympathy that my engine froze up. One of them asked me, "Are you worried about your husband's reaction to you destroying the engine by driving the car with the oil light on?"

My response was that I was not concerned about that because I had already forgiven myself. When I repeated that story to my husband, he said that was one thing he liked about me—how quickly I forgive. He humorously suggested that, in this case, it might have been better if I had waited a little longer to forgive myself.

The power of learning to forgive yourself and others for anything contributing to your unfortunate circumstances is the power of not letting them crush you. I definitely brought the learning I had gleaned about immediately stopping a car when the oil light goes on forward with me into my future. I won't do that again! I dumped the garbage of accusing myself and emotionally abusing myself because of this significant mistake I had made. A crisis is a crisis, but I refuse to make it worse by holding grudges against anyone (including myself) who contributed to it.

Forgiveness is an awesome thing. You may think you are doing it for the other person, but you are actually doing it to bless yourself. By forgiving, you are unloading any negative emotions so you can rationally (and as peacefully as possible) go on with the work of attempting to resolve or adjust to the crisis. Remember that forgiveness is not about excusing or accepting someone else's misbehavior, so much as it is about casting it out of your mind and protecting yourself from allowing their misbehavior to destroy your heart.

Dealing with Depression

When a person has broken through denial and bargaining and faces the true nature of the crisis or loss, the next step of adjustment is often *depression*. The thoughts of, "What could I have done differently?" are replaced with, "Woe is me!"

Depression is when we acknowledge the crisis situation is real and begin to grieve the loss we have experienced (both present and expected future losses). Many people think that grief is a bad thing, but people who never grieve their losses are stuffing emotions that are likely to burst out at inappropriate times or will ultimately emotionally cripple them. It is both okay and necessary to allow yourself to grieve your losses.

My first experience with depression was during my teenage years. The boy that I was going steady with and who was discussing marriage with me found himself attracted to another girl and broke up with me so he could date her. I had a very poor self-concept at the time and this breakup was devastating to me. He rejected me for another girl! This threw me into a deep depression that ended up following me into college.

After becoming a therapist, I could see that I had been clinically depressed over this crisis. At the time I was struggling as a teenager, my thoughts often returned to the loss of him which triggered more depression. I withdrew from others and kept to myself during my freshman year in college. I did not take physical or emotional care of myself. I allowed this depression to last way too long.

One day, it was like I suddenly woke up. I was feeling miserable with depression that day, so miserable that I was fed up with being emotionally sick and tired. A light came on in my mind that I was doing this to myself by dwelling on an unfaithful boy for way too long. He wasn't worth another thought!

I was exhausted from being depressed so long, and I resolved to myself that I would never again allow anyone or any situation in my life to trap me in depressed thinking. I made the decision to not allow thoughts to take up residence in my mind that were not beneficial to me. I cast this boy out of my mind and resumed a happy and full life. I applied this lesson to the remainder of my life. I learned that I could control depression and I would never allow depression to take control of me again!

I also learned another life lesson. When I entered this crisis situation, I thought my life would never be the same again. I allowed my thought life to dwell on the belief that I would never get over this loss. So what really happened? Two years later, I met my husband who was ten times the man that this boy was. My husband was faithful and this boy couldn't measure up in any way to him. Another life lesson for me—a crisis in life can turn out to be a blessing in disguise. I am so happy that I did not marry the boy, because I would never have met my wonderful husband. What a loss that would have been! I wasted many valuable days and much energy in my life believing that I had a devastating loss when I was yet to meet the love of my life.

I am not saying that I never allowed myself to experience depression. Depression is a human emotion that is not harmful if you move on after a brief time of grieving your losses.

I allowed myself to experience my sadness since I was afflicted with cancer and the sometimes agonizing process of going through the treatments needed to deal with it. I knew my emotions were normal and, as a therapist, also knew it was beneficial to allow myself to express my sorrow for a relatively brief period of time.

I knew it was not beneficial for me to agonize over a long period of time, so I would make appointments with myself to allow my feelings to be expressed through sadness and tears. I would give myself an hour to let the emotions all out. When the hour was up, relieved from letting my sadness out, I stopped my grieving and went on to something positive and encouraging in my thoughts. I would then periodically repeat this process as necessary.

I once had someone ask me, "Can you really do that—just decide to grieve for short periods of time and then stop until the next time you need to express your sadness?"

The answer is yes, though, in truth, sometimes your loss will dictate the times when you will grieve. I am not proposing that anyone decide not to express feelings at all with life situations that normally result in sadness. That would be stuffing your feelings which is not beneficial. I am proposing that you can have some control over when you actively grieve and when you give yourself a break.

Don't have this expectation of yourself immediately after suffering the loss. This is a technique that can be very effectively used after the initial shock. Immediately after the shock of a crisis, grieving comes in waves that you do not anticipate and have limited control over. Don't try to stifle that natural emotion (or feel the need to apologize for it) when it occurs during the first month or so following the onset of the crisis.

As you read this today, you may not be okay. You may be grieving and dealing with what seems to be an ocean of sadness. You could be experiencing what it is like to find yourself walking through a time of despair. You might be facing financial struggles, a child or family member who is making troubling choices and breaking your heart, alienation in relationships, a scary diagnosis, persecution and abuse, or any other emotional trauma. You are probably desperate to resolve the deep struggle of your soul, but right now you are just exhausted. Wrestling with this crisis may be draining your strength.

Remember to give yourself breaks from your sadness. One thing that has proven effective for giving me some relief when I find myself in this emotional state is to withdraw for a few hours (or a day) and just sit and have a quiet time. I sit and open the Bible and listen to God during my quiet times. I pray. Many people find encouraging music to be helpful and that is helpful to me as well, especially praise and worship music.

In my case, there is no crisis that God and I cannot face together. I have found him to be the solvent that dissolves the glue that can make me feel stuck in despair. I leave my times with him both hopeful and, maybe even more important, peaceful.

As stated earlier, it is okay to grieve and not be okay for a brief period of time after a crisis. This enables you to say goodby and place that loss behind without staying paralyzed. What is not okay is staying stuck in depression for a long period of time. Some people stay stuck in this stage for years beyond the crisis, and that is neither healthy nor beneficial for them. Seek professional help if you have been frozen in depression. Staying stuck is a choice that you can reverse. If you haven't been able to reverse it on your own, a competent professional therapist or pastoral counselor can help you get unstuck.

When Anger Shows Up

Some people think the next stage in adjustment to loss is not acceptable because it is *anger*. Believe it or not, reaching the adjustment step of anger is beneficial because it pulls the person out of depression and motivates them to move forward.

What is not acceptable to most is not that a person feels anger, but instead it is how they express it. There are healthy outlets for anger. Unfortunately, there are also very unhealthy outlets and those should be avoided or they will likely create a new crisis in your life to add to the one you are already experiencing.

My grandson was traveling on an airplane with me and his stuffed bear, Hudson. He positioned Hudson's face and then told me to look at it. "This is Hudson's angry face!" Caleb declared to me.

I thought, "I know Hudson is inanimate, but he sure does look angry to me ..."

Anger is an emotion we all share, but should never be used to harm another person just because you are hurting. Like the situation with depression, you do not want to allow yourself to get stuck for a prolonged period of time. Seek professional help if you find yourself not letting go of anger within a relatively short period of time or are using forms of expression that are hurting others. Interestingly, holding on to this emotion can be far more harmful to you than it is to others.

Alcoholics Anonymous once taught that not forgiving others is like you drinking poison and hoping it harms the other person. The same is true when you stay angry for an extended period of time. It is not likely to harm them, but certainly is likely to harm you.

I had friends in college who had a unique method of relieving their anger. They would get in their car and drive out into the country where no one would be observing them or concerned about their behavior. They would then step out of the car, jump up and down and scream about their frustration until they tired of this activity, then calmly return to the car, having relieved themselves of the anger. It worked! It was humorous but still a healthy outlet.

People who move through the depression stage quickly may bypass the anger stage because it is not needed to move them on to adjustment. People who have intentionally been hurt by others might find it takes a little longer to pass through the anger stage.

Acceptance of and Adjustment to the Crisis

Acceptance and adjustment come when you no longer need to pretend the crisis did not occur, but are also no longer emotionally disabled by what happened. The crisis happened, and that cannot be changed. It was painful and you suffered because of it, you grieved your loss, but the time has come to let go of the emotional suffering (even if you cannot escape from the physical suffering).

Begin moving forward with the rest of your life. The time has come to stop this crisis from occupying the majority of your thoughts. The moment has arrived when you refuse to let your life stay focused on that crisis even if it is persisting.

> He restores my soul.
> —Psalm 23:3a

When terminal patients reach this step, they determine to get the most out of however much time they have left. Acceptance and adjustment does not mean you do not still seek healing and help from professionals and the God of the impossible, but it does mean that you have allowed him to restore your soul.

I know that, for me, God knows what is ahead of me if I survive longer on earth—I do not. Maybe the best merciful and healing thing our Lord can do is to take me home to be with him. I let him be the one to make that choice and trust his wisdom in the choices he makes for me.

> Abba, Father, for you all things are possible; remove this
> cup from me; yet, not what I want, but what you want.
> —Mark 14:36

In life, we cannot always control what is happening to us. While that may be true, it serves us well to challenge ourselves to exercise some control over how we respond to what is happening. Regardless of the situation, this is the power we have.

This book that you are now reading is an attempt to guide your walk through a crisis with some tools to help you cope—and more than coping—to find the joy and hope that exists even through the darkest corners of despair. In nearly all forms of crises, there are inevitably things which you can and cannot change. In either case, you have everything to gain and nothing to lose by treating yourself to joyful moments in your life and by firmly grasping the hope that enriches every day of the remainder of your life.

> My flesh and my heart may fail,
> but God is the strength of my heart and my portion forever ....
> for me it is good to be near God;
> I have made the LORD GOD my refuge.
> —Psalm 73:26,28

No matter how much it pains us, we cannot have a life that does not have periods of suffering in it interspersed with wonderful journeys of happiness and contentment. We live in a fallen world. No one is immune from the fallout of this situation. Everyone experiences crisis situations which require wisdom and effort in order to prevent them from emotionally disabling us. If you are unhappy with the period of life that you are in now, quite often only patience is required in order to persevere the crisis and regain your zest for life.

> We are afflicted in every way, but not crushed; perplexed,
> but not driven to despair.
> —2Corinthians 4:8

The most unsatisfying position you could choose for yourself is to stay stuck in depression, because it robs you of energy, peace, problem solving abilities, and getting on with your life. It keeps you stuck at the lowest possible point while you are walking through the crisis situation. It creates despair and hopelessness, neither of which facilitates healing. You can experience quietness and calmness through a storm, but not when you choose to stay stuck in depression.

Shane Farmer, senior pastor at Cherry Hills Community Church in Highlands Ranch, Colorado, made this comment in a sermon, "Fire can either destroy or refine. It all depends upon if you waste your pain."

The fire here refers to unpleasant crises in life. We have a choice—will we use this crisis to refine ourselves or will we decide to let it destroy us? Refinement improves our quality of life. I choose refinement!

After a crisis has occurred, your next step is to acknowledge that you have a new reality in your life and then adjust to it. In this book, you will be offered a pattern of responding to life crises and uncertainty which will hopefully maximize your ability to make it through your uncertainty with the least amount of added damage. You may or may not decide to employ some of those methods, but if you fail to employ a strategy of any kind, you will ultimately end up at the mercy of your crisis.

If you are ill and go to a doctor who is able to quickly diagnose what is going wrong in your body and writes you a prescription that should cure the problem, you have a couple of clearly defined choices. You can either take the medicine or not. If you return with your condition unchanged, or even worsened, the doctor would likely ask, "Did you take the medicine that I prescribed for you?"

Your response could be, "I bought the prescription at the pharmacist and took the prescription home with me."

The doctor would probably respond, "But did you take the medicine inside the bottle?"

You retort, "I read the prescription three times a day like it said on the bottle."

The doctor would then surely declare, "I am not asking whether you faithfully read the prescription. I am asking whether you actually took the medicine? You can't get well by just reading the prescription. You must do what it says to do."

We can spend hours and hours reading many books on how to get our life back into balance with our new realities, but we won't experience the healing they offer unless we do more than just read the books. We need to put the new information and guidance they give us into action before a transformation will take place to ease our present discomfort. We need to do more than just read the prescription. We must also make necessary changes in our reactions or else our prescription will just sit on the shelf, unable to cure us until we swallow the pill.

That is true of all uncertainty we may be dealing with. Educating yourself on the most productive responses to devastating crises is a good first step. However, if you do nothing to change your behavior or attitude, there will likely be no change (or even a negative change) in your condition.

When you are willing to actually change your outlook and behavior is when you have the best chance of finding contentment and joy in your life. It is also when you have the best chance of resolving the crisis situation.

Sometimes we decide to hang on to unproductive or counterproductive behaviors. There is a certain amount of insanity in stubbornly holding on to unproductive or damaging mindsets when they are not working in helping you journey through a crisis. Doing more of the same things that have been intensifying or not resolving the crisis cannot be expected to help you achieve healing and/or walk you out of the crisis. It is very interesting how often, when our distress is increasing, that we think we can continue making the same harmful choices and somehow expect different results.

Overcoming Negativity

I love something my pastor, Shane Farmer, said in a recent sermon, "If you want to slay giants you will have to overcome fear and negativity. Courage is the antidote to fear. The greatest regrets you will have in life will be the lions you didn't chase, and the giants you avoided."

The uncertainty you are living with is like a giant in your life. You can respond with either fear or courage when this giant shows up. In the Bible, David responded to Goliath with courage, blessing innumerable others in the process. You will bless all those you love and who love you when you choose courage in the face of uncertainty! You will also bless yourself in the process.

> When you pass through the waters, I will be with you.
> —Isaiah 43:2a

Let us now look at seven steps which can help you make it through a life crisis without losing your joy, hope, enjoyment, and enthusiasm for life. If you are reading this, you do have at least some life ahead of you. None of us have a promise for how long that will be, but attitude affects whether that time will be dreary or dear. Each of these steps will be discussed more fully in subsequent chapters.

Steps for Seeking the Best Outcome of a Crisis Situation:

1. *Keep a positive attitude.* Sometimes, when you expect the worst to happen, you facilitate its occurrence. Choosing to keep your focus fixed on the losses from your crisis (to the exclusion of focusing on the positive aspects that are still in your life despite it) is making a bad situation worse. When we are in a difficult situation, the last thing we want to do is to make it worse. Allow yourself to schedule joy, peace, hope, and optimism breaks into your life to counteract the power that the difficult situation wants to steal from you. Let your attitude be a positive attitude. Know that the power of most crisis situations is temporary. Also know that despite the difficult circumstances that might be facing you or your loved one, you can still have a peaceful life during your remaining tenure on this earth. Assume you can courageously face your future and still find quality and

happiness on this earth to counteract the problems you are passing through.

2. *Seek spiritual healing.* The spirit of people is at the core of their very being. A healthy spirit gives the bearings to cope with or resolve a crisis situation peacefully. Experiencing the peace that passes understanding in the midst of walking through a crisis rests in spiritual healing. In cancer, studies have found that people who are spiritually connected have the highest cure rates. In any crisis, being spiritually focused will predispose you to the best outcome possible under the circumstances you find yourself in. Trust God when you do not trust yourself or the difficulty you are passing through. You have everything to gain and nothing to lose by doing this. Situations can seem impossible to us, but always remember that:

For mortals it is impossible, but for God all
things are possible.
—Matthew 19:26b

3. *Take your focus off of the problem. Focus on solutions instead.* Those who keep their focus fixed on the problem feel frustrated and helpless and become depressed. People who focus instead on feasible solutions are more positive, hopeful, and encouraged as they experiment with various possible solutions to help them effectively pass through the crisis. Educate yourself and seek wise counsel before deciding how best to react to a crisis situation. Determine which option gives you the best opportunity to get through it with minimal losses. The more choices you come up with to deal with and attempt to resolve your difficult passage (or your emotional reaction to it), the better your chances are that you will come up with a really great, effective choice.

4. *Be hopeful.* Never give up hope. This is so important, I will repeat it once more. Never give up hope! Hope sustains us

during crisis periods. Hope is choosing to focus on a positive outcome of the uncertain situation itself or a positive outcome after the uncertainty has passed. Hope can actually change the outcome in a very positive way. It does not matter whether those around you are hopeful. Don't allow anyone to discourage you from having hope. People who are draining you of hope are toxic and working against recovery. Don't let them steal your hope. Give yourself permission to limit your contact with toxic people while you are passing through your crisis. If your crisis is a health crisis which has become terminal on this earth, let your hope be in the future—that you will be transitioning from this earth to eternal life where love endures and no one can take your joy or hope away from you.

5. *Don't isolate yourself.* We benefit when we walk through our crisis with wise advisors, family, and friends. Love and hugs from others are a powerful healing balm. Really! Isolation is a result of depression and depression is debilitating. Depression steals joy and peace from your life as you give into the hopelessness it offers. Isolation can lead you into an outcome of the crisis that you do not want to insert into your life. Isolation is a choice to make a bad situation worse by keeping your focus fixed on yourself and your suffering instead of experiencing the fullness of life that comes from turning your focus off of yourself and onto others. You must take care of yourself in times of chaos, but you must also take time to express love to those around you.

6. *Avoid becoming self-centered.* Again, take your focus off of yourself and put it on others. When you focus on bringing healing into other people's lives, you bring healing into your own life. This may seem very difficult to do when you are in pain, but self-centeredness robs you of hope and healing. The more focused on self that you allow yourself to become, the greater the chance you will drive yourself into a deep state of depression. Like they say in drug abuse prevention, "Just say

no!" Just say no to keeping your focus fixed on yourself (poor me, I don't deserve this) and just say no to allowing yourself to stay depressed. The consequence you get from expecting others to constantly be there to meet your needs is that they shy away from you and allow you to wallow in the depravity of your self-centeredness. You and your crisis are not the gravitational center around which the world and the people in it should be revolving. That is an unreal expectation.

7. *Keep your sense of humor.* If you haven't had a good sense of humor, this would be a good time to develop one. Cancer studies, among others, have shown that laughter has a healing effect on the body. It will protect you from going crazy while you are passing through your crisis, but it can also be effective in crisis management. I remember when I was in graduate school, studying to become a counselor, I stated to my professors that I wanted to start a new type of therapy called "laughter therapy." That was my reaction to observing people allowing themselves to become more self-absorbed and needy as they were passing through crisis situations. Later in life, I went to a humor workshop which asked the question, "What do you do to allow yourself to find something to laugh about every day?" I will now pose that question to you. Challenge yourself to find something to laugh about every day. If you can find something about yourself to laugh at, all the better!

CHAPTER 2

Releasing the Joy Trapped Within

Your Joy is Still There—You Just Need to Find It!

A cheerful heart is a good medicine,
but a downcast spirit dries up the bones.
—Proverbs 17:22

For who wishes anything for any other reason than that
he may become happy? There is no man who does not
desire this, and each one desires it with such earnestness
that he prefers it to all other things; whoever, in fact,
desires other things, desires them for this end alone.
—Augustine

I know that there is nothing better for them than to be
happy and enjoy themselves as long as they live.
—Ecclesiastes 3:12

Many of us struggle to find a dream that doesn't turn
out to be a nightmare. Or we find ourselves shipwrecked
when our dreams come true, but they turn out nothing
like we thought they would. We have come to the place
that we think of every human as pre-great. The world
needs you to find the hero within you. Most of us don't
choose the worst life, we just don't choose the best. The

world needs you at your best. This planet is made better or worse by the people we choose to become. If you live a diminished life, it's not only you who loses, but the world loses, and humanity loses. There is a story to be written by your life, it is a heroic tale. Though you may not recognize it, there is greatness within you.
—Erwin Raphael McManus, *Wide Awake*

Erwin Raphael McManus in his book, *Wide Awake,* explains that in the midst of a life crisis, we are encouraged to not be stuck there. Instead, he encourages us to create a great future for ourselves and those we love, despite setbacks due to uncertainty in our lives.

To create a different world is both a courageous act and a creative act. Life is a work of art. The canvas you paint first is your life. Then your life becomes the brush from which you paint that part of the world you touch while you are here on this planet. You are an artist. What work of art will you leave behind?

Some spend their time painting images that only remember the past. Their dreams are a memorial to what was. Others live in regret and dream of only of what could have been. Still, there are those who dream of a world that does not yet exist; of a world that must exist. They dream a future that must be created. They are the artists of that future.

Creating the life of your dreams begins with the dream. It begins with the ability to imagine yourself differently than you are and your life differently than it is.
—Erwin Raphael McManus, *Wide Awake*

Be an Artist

Do you want to be the artist that paints a beautiful mural born of courage and creativity, or do you want to hand over your canvas for others to scribble on and destroy? Do you want to paint vibrant colors into the world around you, or do you want your crisis to obliterate your mural from view?

Artists who focus on their end goal produce the most wonderful works of art. They cover over their mistakes by painting new successes over their prior failures. Most artists are courageous, creative, innovative, and want to leave behind a beautiful and joyful work of art for others to enjoy. It is interesting how often these artists encourage themselves at the same time they are trying to encourage others.

When anxiety was great within me, your consolation brought joy to my soul.
Psalm 94:19

> Rejoice in hope, be patient in suffering, persevere in prayer.
> —Romans 12:12

> A cheerful heart has a continual feast.
> —Proverbs 15:15b

As a mental health therapist, I often found myself helping people who were trying to navigate through the splintered remains of their lives, after slamming into an unexpected detour.

Did I mention that I don't like detours? They are no fun and so full of uncertainties that people find themselves overwhelmed by the thought of the strange new roads they are being forced upon. Thoughts like these may cross our minds: "Do I find someone who looks like they know where they are going and follow them? What if they really don't know where they are going and they lead me to a dead end? Backtracking takes up so much time and is so frustrating!"

When your life circumstances have placed you on an emotional roller coaster, you still have choices. You may not have the choice to exit the roller coaster until it stops, but you do have control over how you choose to respond to being stuck there for the duration. You can be terrified and increase your trauma, or you can lift your hands into the air and pretend it is the ride of your life. Pretending is okay if it makes the ride a little less traumatic.

Some people enjoy roller coasters, others do not. However, no rational person desires the emotional loops and rolls that come with traumatic circumstances. For some people, roller coaster rides are something they actively seek to replace tedium with thrills. In the case of a crisis, we inevitably resent the roller coaster that we find ourselves on. It is not unusual to feel trauma at just the thought of boarding that roller coaster.

That is often true of people with sudden illness striking them or their loved ones. It is equally true with others who unexpectedly experience great losses or crises in life. This could be a loss of a job; loss of a relationship; loss of health; financial ruin; death of parent, spouse, child or dear friend; suicide; Alzheimer's; overwhelming losses; Parkinson's; or any other significant crisis or loss in our life.

> So you have pain now; but I will see you again, and your hearts will rejoice, and no one will take your joy from you.
> —John 16:22

> *How to gain, how to keep, how to recover happiness, is in fact for most men at all times the secret motive of all they do, and all they are willing to endure.*
> —William James

Focusing on Others Instead of Self

I had a dear friend, Tom, who I had the privilege of walking with as he was passing through his journey with inoperable brain cancer. Tom's cancer was loss number one. His wife left him because she could not handle this new found trauma. Casualty number two. After the cancer progressed in his brain, he lost his ability to continue working and he began to lose his independence. Defeat number three. Several years later he was losing his ability to walk and was starting to experience nausea and dizziness as a result of the progression of his disease. Forfeiture number four. Initially his cancer diagnosis included a prognosis of six months or less of expected survival. Seven years later, the cancer eventually became terminal and he found himself in a hospice for palliative care. Penalty number five. What impact do you think this debilitating disease had on Tom?

Tom was not a quitter—he was a fighter—and he never quit fighting for living the most meaningful and productive life he could. He kept his focus fixed on God and anyone within his reach that needed either encouragement or love. No one died alone while Tom was in the hospice. He went from room to room to meet his fellow patients. He spent the time to get to know them well, and then to become their encourager as their life was ebbing away. If they were alone while they were actively dying, he would go to their room and remain with them until their last breath. It was important to Tom that no one within his reach died alone.

No one knows what it is like to walk through a specific crisis as well as someone who has passed through that type of a situation. Tom knew how difficult it was to be told that his disease was progressing to the point of actively dying—that his tenure on earth was about to end. This is difficult information for anyone to receive. It was certainly as difficult for him as it would have been for someone else. Tom knew how it felt to be abandoned in the midst of pain. With his life reaching its end, Tom grabbed his paint brush and added one more masterly stroke to his mural. He became the one who cared for lonely people, holding their hand as their life ebbed away. Tom took a mural filled with dark edges of disappointment, fear, pain, and loss. He painted over it a poignant final fresco.

Tom kept a sense of purpose in his life, even while passing through the final stage of degeneration. He would not let the focus of his life be on his own suffering. He took his focus off of himself and found peace in providing relief for others in the final stage of their distress. A curious thing happens when people take the focus off of themselves and put it onto others. Sharing in other's pain and suffering doubles down on peace for both parties through the act of love. It gives a precious sense of purpose in the midst of the crisis. It gives respite to everyone involved, both the nurturer and the nurtured.

One particular example of this in Tom's final days was a woman he came to know who loved baseball, yet had never been to a major league game. Tom had enjoyed attending Colorado Rockies games together with his friends. At one game, a player gave Tom an autographed jersey.

Once Tom heard of this woman's love of baseball, he went to his room and came back bearing two gifts. In one hand he had two game tickets he had recently received, and in the other hand he had the autographed jersey (autographed, as it so happens, by one of the woman's favorite players). He deprived himself of these two prized possessions, and he gave them to her for the joy of seeing the respite it provided from her suffering. She went to the game and for the remaining weeks of her life, she treasured the demonstration of love that Tom had shown her. Her family repeatedly told Tom how much his sacrifice meant to them and to her.

Why did Tom reach out to this woman when he, too, was dying? He did it for the joy of bringing happy moments into the life of another person who, like him, was in the process of leaving this life to go to a better eternal life. He considered every remaining possession a gift from God to be shared with those that God brought him into relationship with. Because his focus was not on himself and his suffering, he still experienced joy despite his progressive disease. He decided that the remainder of his life would be lived to its fullest, bringing joy to other patients who (like himself) had limited time left on the earth. Bringing them joy brought him joy! *He learned the secret of living a joy-filled life despite unfavorable circumstances.*

There is truth in the statement that belief produces behavior. Tom did an excellent job of believing that he could still have joy and purpose in his remaining days. Not only could he experience joy, but he could bring joy into the lives of his fellow sufferers in that hospice. He firmly believed that truth, and this belief produced the behavior that brought joy to himself and others. Tom girded his soul as his body withered.

Tom believed that Jesus would live up to all the promises that he gives those who believe in him, love him, and give him lordship over their lives. Tom trusted that his Lord would be with him and comfort him as he prepared to meet Christ face to face. Tom, in the midst of dying, transitioned from this life to the eternal one. While that transition is imperfect on earth, I am confident that it has been perfected for Tom in his death. I sincerely look forward to enjoying my precious friend again, when my tenure on this earth ends.

> Do not let your hearts be troubled. Believe in God, believe also in me. In my Father's house there are many dwelling places. If it were not so, would I have told you that I go to prepare a place for you? And if I go and prepare a place for you, I will come again and will take you to myself, so that where I am, there you may be also. And you know the way to the place where I am going.
> —John 14:1–4

For God so loved the world that he gave his only Son,
so that everyone who believes in him may not perish but
may have eternal life.
—John 3:16

The Power of Joy

I had another friend named Bill who was a veteran of the Vietnam war. Bill was one of the happiest people I have ever known. I loved him deeply and he loved me and others deeply. Despite the trauma he had suffered in his lifetime, Bill decided to forgo hatred, replacing it with compassion. Bill had some terrific reasons to hate.

It started when he was born. Bill was a precious black man, yet his early life was filled with prejudice due to the color of his skin. It is hard for someone who has not lived with racism to understand how demeaning and damaging it is to a person. This was crisis number one for Bill and it was a crisis he was born into.

During the Vietnam war, Bill was a soldier who was captured and became a POW: prisoner of war. Talk about a life crisis! He described what life was like there. His meals were the same every day—rice patties and water. He and the other prisoners were placed in solitary confinement and not allowed to see or talk to each other—though they eventually learned to communicate by tapping on the walls.

Intermittently, a Viet Cong soldier would come to his cell, pull him out and beat him, then throw him back into his cell. When Bill heard feet drawing near to his cell, he never knew if it would be for food or a beating. When they were not beating him, he had to listen to them beating other soldiers. They weren't being punished because they misbehaved—they were being beat because they were Americans.

And when Bill returned home from the war? It was not the same America that in recent decades supported returning soldiers. The

Vietnam war was unpopular back home and support for its veterans was not nearly as absolute as it should have been. Returning soldiers now receive treatment for PTSD: post-traumatic stress disorder. That particular diagnosis was not as understood in Bill's day as it is today. Veterans (even those who suffered through the daily horror of POW status) were largely left to figure out how to reengage in society on their own once they returned home.

Some people learn to hate when they undergo unkind, demeaning, or unfair treatment. But not Bill. Bill learned to love despite his circumstances and while that love did not come cheap, it benefited him for the remainder of his life. Bill's love and joy was infectious to all who had the pleasure of knowing him well. Those who were blessed by being in Bill's presence felt joy at having him in their lives. He had a hopeful and resourceful spirit.

Bill loved to sing and couldn't stop his body from moving to and fro with the melody. He joined our church choir and was beloved by choir members and our congregation. He was a source of joy to the people around him. It was as though every cell in his body enjoyed life! Bill increased our enjoyment of life simply by being himself. Very few people knew the suffering Bill encountered in his walk through life. He didn't talk about it unless asked. They wouldn't have suspected that a man who had been so significantly mistreated could ever be so loving and joyful.

I once asked Bill how he made it through his time in solitary confinement as a POW. Bill was a Christian and said his faith kept him intact. He replied that he considered how much Christ had suffered for him and he didn't consider his suffering as anything compared to that. How could he be angry over what others had done, if he was under the grace of someone who had suffered immeasurably more?

Bill would not let his spirit be defeated by his unfavorable situation. The enemy could attack him mercilessly, but even when the enemy had power over his body, he would not give them power over his mind and spirit. He survived like this for seven years before he was released at the end of the Vietnam war. Seven years of isolation, random beatings, just enough food to stay alive, and being surrounded by hate from the Viet Cong. He had years of experience in looking away from the trauma in his life and focusing instead on the joy and hope that he guarded in his heart—a joy and hope that no one could steal from him.

Many former POWs suffered from extreme PTSD for years after their release, if not for a lifetime. Bill did not. Even when, years after his release, he developed permanent respiratory problems (caused by the diet of rice patties) he would not yield his emotions to negative outcomes. He was still singing and moving with the music in his body and his spirit. He remained full of joy and hope. His focus was fixed on what was positive and good in his life. Bill stubbornly refused to focus on the negatives that had beset his life, recognizing that in doing so he would be causing himself further losses. What an amazing and life enhancing choice he made! This same choice is available to all of us.

What saved Bill from being emotionally crippled for the rest of his life? His joy could not be dampened by adverse circumstances. He took his focus off of himself and put it on God, then proceeded through life with the peace and joy that passes understanding—and surely passes the somber life crises he had been through.

> The Lord is near. Do not worry about anything, but in everything by prayer and supplication with thanksgiving let your requests be made known to God. And the peace of God, which surpasses all understanding, will guard your hearts and your minds in Christ Jesus.
> —Philippians 4:5b–7

> My soul is satisfied as with a rich feast,
> and my mouth praises you with joyful lips ...
> for you have been my help,
> and in the shadow of your wings I sing for joy.

> My soul clings to you;
> your right hand upholds me.
> —Psalm 63:5,7–8

One thing that each of the previously discussed people had in common was that they used their stored up joy and a sense of humor to keep them focused on the good things in life, despite the devastating impact of the life crisis they were walking through. They stubbornly refused to give in to feelings of defeat and instead looked for and found enjoyable moments and themes in their lives. They decided to emotionally dwell in the protected spaces which brought them (and others) joy.

They chose to keep their thoughts fixed on God and on the positive aspects that remained in their lives and relationships. They made an active choice to give themselves relief from their pain. They made another active choice to keep themselves from being trapped in the negative aspects of problems. They chose hope instead of despair; joy instead of depression; as well as life and finding enjoyment in the remainder of their lives over allowing their crisis to steal their peace. They eliminated doomsday predictions from their thoughts. They chose to dwell on hopeful thoughts. They discovered the truth that you can exercise control over your thoughts.

> Finally, beloved, whatever is true, whatever is honorable, whatever is just, whatever is pure, whatever is pleasing, whatever is commendable, if there is any excellence and if there is anything worthy of praise, think about these things.
> —Philippians 4:8

Keeping your joy despite your present circumstances is not dependent on perfect circumstances. Happiness and joy are often thought of as being two separate things. It has become somewhat controversial recently whether happiness and joy are just synonyms for each other or have separate meanings. They do truly overlap each other, but some differences can be noted.

Be Happy

> *Man is unable not to wish to be happy.*
> —Thomas Aquinas

Thomas Aquinas writes that the pursuit of happiness is an unalterable aspect of humanity. We cannot help from wanting to be happy and we will pursue many things in order to attempt to obtain it. While our own mental outlook affects our ability to obtain it, life circumstances can intrude to make this pursuit more or less challenging to achieve.

Let's take a look at what happiness is. *Happiness is often defined as an emotion that occurs when your life is going well.* Many psychological, philosophical, and spiritual approaches have striven to define happiness in order to help us understand where the emotional state of happiness comes from. Biological studies have also been conducted on the body's role in happiness. Various research groups have applied the scientific method to answer questions about happiness and how a person experiences it.

Many definitions of happiness include descriptions like these: contentment; a sense of well being; the emotional reaction to encountering positive events; an emotional response when being accepted, loved or complimented by others; satisfaction; euphoria; experiencing pleasure; spiritually feeling blessed; and being satisfied with one's life. The underpinning of happiness is that life is going well. Therefore, your life conditions usually need to be positive in order to experience happiness.

Rarely, but sometimes, you encounter a person who is basically happy regardless of life events. That person is not happy about the crisis situation, but is happy in other areas of life and does not allow a crisis to dissipate happiness.

It is probably an understatement to say that all people desire happiness and give attaining it a high priority in their lives. People speculate on what brings about happiness, and different people would give different responses as to what they think would make their lives happier. My oncologist once told me that happiness plays an important role in one's physical health and that in his experience, happy people live longer than unhappy people.

Since happiness is often seen coming as a result of very favorable circumstances, it is not considered consistent or enduring. According to this definition, happiness comes and goes according to the life situation you find yourself in. When everything is going the way you want it to go, you are happy. When unpleasant surprises occur, happiness is dissipated.

> The art of being happy lies in the power of extracting happiness from common things.
> —Henry Ward Beecher.

Remember the great things that you have in your life that are still there despite your crisis situation. Some of those things can be your family, fun recreational opportunities, being with friends, finding ways to enjoy life like a young child would do, the beauty of nature, the companionship of a pet, etc. Keep your focus on the positive aspects of your life. Find ways to still enjoy life despite your crisis. Look for new adventures!

When you are experiencing a life crisis, unless you are a very unusual person, you will not be happy about the circumstance you find yourself in. Did you know that you can experience joy even when you are not happy about the adverse circumstances in your life? It is all about focus. If you keep your focus fixed on your unfortunate circumstances, you will be hurling yourself over a cliff of impending deep depression. If you choose to focus on your blessings, you will be making a choice to experience joy despite the crisis. For me, I keep my gaze on Christ and his many blessings in my life—which include my family and my friends. This gives me immense joy despite any adverse circumstances life throws at me.

High Emotions Cloud Rational Thinking

While teaching Developmental Psychology to college students, I came across studies which indicated that physiological changes in a highly emotional state have a mathematically inverse relationship to those in a rational state. An inverse relationship means that as one goes up, the other goes down, a little bit like being on a see saw. Simply put, this means that the more emotional we are when facing decisions in life, the less rational we are.

If we are being flooded by emotions, making good rational decisions becomes increasingly more challenging. A fallout from trying to resolve problems or arguments in a highly charged state is that we have a tendency to escalate the discord instead of resolving the original problem. When the intense time is over and we return to a more rational time, we now are dealing with not only the original crisis, but also the fallout from inflammatory words spoken or actions taken while we were in a heightened emotional state.

This can be boiled down even more concisely. While you are emotional, don't try problem-solving. Wait until you have returned to a calmer, more rational state. By doing this, you will increase the chances that your efforts will result in a productive outcome.

Joy is Being Exceedingly Glad

Biblically, the word "joy" comes from the Greek root word chara and means "to be exceedingly glad." *The great thing about joy is that we can experience joy when life is not going so well.* Now, let's look at what joy is.

Joy is a feeling of great pleasure and delight which is not dependent on positive life circumstances. Joy involves a decision to enjoy one's life despite finding oneself in an unpleasant life crisis. Joy is cheerfulness, a spiritual reaction to having God and other loved ones in your life, an emotion that surprisingly often shows up even in adverse circumstances. Joy isn't always an automatic function based on what has occurred in your life, but *it is the result of what and how you choose to think.*

I was greatly encouraged by the following wise words when I was passing through my greatest life crisis to date. Hope they encourage you also ...

> For they will scarcely brood over the days of their lives, because God keeps them occupied with the joy of their hearts.
> —Ecclesiastes 5:20

> Though the fig tree does not blossom,
> and no fruit is on the vines;
> though the produce of the olive fails,
> and the fields yield no food;
> though the flock is cut off from the fold,
> and there is no herd in the stalls,
> yet I will rejoice in the LORD;
> I will exult in the God of my salvation.
> God, the Lord, is my strength.
> —Habakkuk 3:17–19a

> *Life isn't about waiting for the storm to pass. It's about learning to dance in the rain.*
> —Unknown

Jovial people laugh a lot and are thankful for the sweet relationships and blessings in their life. It is here that we can define joy as being more than happiness. Cheerful individuals are not easily offended and they are loving. Joy gives a person hope. Upbeat people are more focused on others than on themselves.

> For everything there is a season, and a time for every matter under heaven ....
> a time to weep, and a time to laugh;

> a time to mourn, and a time to dance.
> —Ecclesiastes 3:1,4

As I stated earlier, my current crisis is cancer. The process of waiting for an original diagnosis felt surreal—could this really be happening to me? After the diagnosis, my pastor and his wife reminded me that denial was not such a terrible thing. They were suggesting that I could choose to not make cancer the *focus* of my life, even though it was *in* my life. They weren't implying that I not accept the reality of this disease. They were recommending that I give myself mental breaks from that reality.

> So do not worry about tomorrow, for tomorrow will bring worries of its own. Today's trouble is enough for today.
> —Matthew 6:34

My dad was also a model that helped me through this period, even though he had left this earth several years earlier. He was a joyful man and an optimist at heart. My mother began moving more fully into dementia as he began his decline due to congestive heart failure. He was in his own life crisis, but consistently helped her when she was confused—which was happening more frequently as he was declining.

Paranoia can enter into the challenging picture of dementia, and even when she was exhibiting this trait with him, he continued to walk through this period with her without viewing her in a negative light. He did not complain, even to his children, about those new challenges in his life. He sought out funny TV shows for breaks from his new reality with those challenges. He would not allow the oppressive situation to steal his zest!

As he was in his final months of life, I was touched by how gracefully he moved through the process of needing to be put on oxygen and then in a wheelchair. He was a very independent man, but I never heard him complain of the significant changes in his life. I asked him how he made those changes so gracefully and he responded that *we have limited control over what our body does to us, but we do have control over our attitude and adjustment to those changes.* Those words became very comforting to me and a model for my walk through the uncertainties of cancer, even though he was no longer here.

My daughter, Michelle, is an amazing model of a person who adamantly refuses to let a life crisis shake her pleasant, joyful, optimistic demeanor. I want to be more like her. I pray that God will keep her that way and grow me more like her. Some people take the lemons that come in life and make lemonade out of them. She and my daughter-in-law, Belle, are two of those people. I am not crazy about lemons, but I do like lemonade. What a gift it is to be able to take something that is sour in life and turn it into something that is pleasant. I want that gift! I am working at developing that skill in my life ...

Creative Approaches to Regain Courage

The constructive approach is to become more creative in how to overcome the negative emotional effects of the crisis in order to best deal with this disruption in your life.

Another way to look at an extreme crisis in your life is to look at it as an opportunity. That would be a dramatic change in how you look at it, wouldn't it? Think of how differently you would be able to approach the problem if, instead of being emotionally defeated by it, you would see it as an opportunity to grow, to be innovative, to be courageous, to be patient, to be brave, to trust people who are trying to help you through the crisis, to overcome negative emotions, and to prevail over the crisis. Then go even a step further by visualizing what this walk through the uncertain challenge would be like if you adamantly refused to let it steal your joy. You don't have to be happy about the crisis to continue to feel joy in spite of it!

The surprising element of happiness research is that our circumstances only account for ten percent of our happiness. The most joyful people may be living through terrible life circumstances and the least cheerful may be living through amazing circumstances.

In other words, *being thankful for what you do have—even in the midst of your crisis—increases joy.* When you focus on what you are grateful for, you are taking your attention off of what you are unhappy about and putting it instead on what brings you joy. Try taking your focus off of you and your unfortunate situation and put it on acts of kindness. This is an area that the Bible taught about and modern scientific theory agrees with. Charity is as much a gift to the giver as it is to the person in need. When you are hurt by people and situations, holding grudges will only destroy happiness.

Forgive for Your Peace

> Forgive others not because they deserve forgiveness, but because you deserve peace.
> —Jonathan Lockwood Huie, *Simply an Inspired Life*

> Forgiveness is an act of the will, and the will can function regardless of the temperature of the heart.
> —Corrie Ten Boom with Jamie Buckingham, *Tramp for the Lord*

Excuse people and situations which have emotionally wounded you so that you can move forward with a joy filled life. The Bible teaches the importance of pardoning others and scientific studies now support the relationship between forgiving and reclaiming happiness. *Joy does not just show up at your door in a crisis situation. It occurs as a result of your attitudes and the active choices you make to not let your crisis destroy your joy.*

> Whenever you stand praying, forgive, if you have
> anything against anyone.
> —Mark 11:25a

> Bear with one another and, if anyone has a complaint
> against another, forgive each other; just as the Lord has
> forgiven you, so you also must forgive. Above all, clothe
> yourselves with love, which binds everything together
> in perfect harmony. And let the peace of Christ rule in
> your hearts, to which indeed you were called in the one
> body. And be thankful.
> —Colossians 3:13–15

Forgiving others does not mean that you do not set safe boundaries around yourself to protect yourself from emotional or physical abuse. Some people may be so negative in their behavior and attitudes that they bring you down just by being in their presence. These people are toxic to someone who is trying to overcome a difficult emotional crisis and it is okay to decide that you need a time out from them. You can forgive someone and still avoid spending time with them if they are interfering with your healing. But if you must do this, do it gently for a restricted period of time and never allow unkind words to leave your mouth. More importantly, never allow unkind or retaliatory thoughts to enter your mind. They won't enter your lips if you do not allow them to enter your heart and mind.

Avoid Assumptions

At all costs, avoid assumptions. Sometimes it is not the other person in your life that is hurting you. You may be making assumptions about them having negative feelings or criticisms about you when they, in truth, do not. You may be conjuring this up in your imagination and believing something about them that is not true. Assumptions mixed with paranoia can be a precarious combination. If there is ever a time in your life that it is important to quit imagining the worst, it is now. You don't need to add that grief to your heart when you are already in crisis over something else.

The problem when people make negative assumptions is that they begin to accept them as fact. They may be very erroneous. Another aspect about assumptions is that once they begin to be negative, they can multiply very quickly, so that a simple miscommunication can quickly spiral (in our minds) into a great offense. A crisis situation is bad enough in and of itself. Don't increase your pain by making negative assumptions about others and giving yourself something new to grieve about in addition to the crisis.

One of the best New Year's resolutions my husband and I made years ago was to quit making assumptions about people or their motives, then treating them like facts. We had, over time, discovered that many of our assumptions were wrong and rarely beneficial in developing healthy and fulfilling relationships. When we think too much, we are most likely to create a problem that isn't actually there. This is especially true if we let our negative thoughts run amuck in our minds. The only way to clean house of those thoughts is to not allow them residence in our minds.

Pray for those who have hurt you and ask God to teach you how to love them. Don't drink the poison of discontentment. Ask God to grow your love for them and their love for you. I know that while I have been going through this crisis with cancer, unkind words or accusations wound me more deeply than they could ever have wounded me before. It is very difficult and sometimes feels impossible to cast those hurtful words forever from our mind. When you are gathering together every resource you have to mobilize a positive focus which promotes healing for self and others, you are fragile.

Our focus is on bringing joy into our lives and the lives of others, but sometimes we momentarily fail at that. We hope others will forgive us when we fail, so we need also to excuse them when they fail. We also pray that through the act of forgiveness, we can eliminate the wounds of ill-thought-out words from others and avoid damaging ourselves again by recalling and reliving them.

Remember who you are. Don't let others define who you are by their negative interpretation of you. Always remember your positive characteristics. Be willing to grow and change as a result of valid input you receive. Forget negative input that is not valid. By doing this, you can become the best version of you possible! Don't let anyone stop you from doing that!

> Your value doesn't decrease based on someone's inability
> to see your worth.
> —Unknown

> If you find happiness, people may be jealous. Be happy
> anyway.
> —based on poems by Kent M Kieth and
> Mother Teresa's *Anyway* poem

Set some goals for yourself—positive goals—life affirming goals. Goals to enrich your life and the lives of those around you. *Almost no one would want to set a goal of spending the rest of their lives miserable. Even worse is the idea that others around you should be miserable too, just because of your crisis. The result of setting positive and achievable goals is that it makes you more joyful despite the struggles you find yourself entangled in.* Some people will compound their misery by resenting those who overcome similar struggles in a joyful manner.

If you harbor a toxic attitude regarding your struggles, it poisons the air for everyone around you. While it sometimes seems that misery loves company, in truth, misery makes a wretched companion. Do not set a goal for yourself that compounds agony. Do not make the mistake of thinking that you will find relief in the presence of unhappy people. You will only find the amplification of your own unfortunate circumstances.

The route that provides the most relief is searching for and finding whatever scraps of joy remain, even in the midst of the worst moments of suffering. You might be surprised how these cumulative scraps can make for a feast.

The Healing Power of Laughter

As I am writing this portion of the book, I am at a retreat. I recommend retreats—a time to just relax and give your heart, soul and mind a chance to renew itself. Last night was great medicine for the soul. As we were playing a domino game, we laughed and laughed and laughed. One of the people playing with us who was going through a life crisis declared, "We need more laughter in our lives!"

While serious situations are serious situations, we do not need to remain insufferably somber when we go through them. Interspersing laughter is good medicine. In fact, scientific research has shown that laughter is a curative agent to the body. It appears to mobilize the immune system to help you in fighting illnesses. It has also been proven beneficial in fighting a serious illness like cancer.

Laughter elevates one's spirit and clears the emotional cobwebs so we can think more clearly. It creates a friendly environment for our immune system to build itself up to fight disease. On the other hand, being overly stressed breaks down the immune system and provides fertile ground for disease to thrive and grow in.

When I was going through a tough round of systemic therapy, my nurse practitioner came in to visit with me. She declared to me that my sense of humor was what was going to get me through the treatments. She said that without a sense of humor, this type of treatment could drive one crazy. It appears that laughter can keep you sane and stop you from mentally going off the deep end when adverse chemicals are being poured into your body through your bloodstream.

The chemicals used in my body made it bloat up until I was unrecognizable when I looked into a mirror. I couldn't change the physical impact on my body, but I would not yield my mind and spirit to them. I chose to laugh at what I saw in the mirror instead of being terrorized by it. I was counting on this just being a temporary effect, which it was. Even if it had been a permanent effect, my response would be to adjust to it. Again, I had no logical choice but to yield my body to the chemicals that had been placed in it. I stubbornly refuse to yield my mind and spirit to despair.

Don't water the weeds in your life by focusing on them. Negative thoughts are like weeds in your life. Who wants to look at gnarly weeds when the opportunity for planting and enjoying flowers gives us so much more pleasure? Most people work hard to get rid of weeds. Remember that pulling up weeds is easier as they start growing. It is more difficult to pull up a weed after it is well rooted.

Don't water the weeds in your life by focusing on them. The sooner you recognize you have weeds and begin pulling them out of your life, the easier it is to rid yourself of those ugly emotional weeds. Hopelessness or emotionally devastating thoughts are the weeds of our lives that we want to pull out as early as they appear. Don't let them grow until their roots are deep and they are difficult to get rid of. You can still eliminate them when their roots are deep, but it takes much more effort to do so than if you get rid of them as they start growing and have shallow roots. Rip them out of the ground before they flourish!

I once saw a church sign that said, "A bad attitude is like a flat tire. You don't go anywhere until you change it."

When is the last time you had a good laugh? A really deep belly laugh? Treat yourself to one! Find the funniest video you can find and watch it and just let yourself get lost in hilarity. It not only makes you feel better, it is healthy for the heart, body, and soul.

When was the last time that you allowed yourself to delight in doing something? You may not have the energy for a fun run, but you can always find something enjoyable to do if you will just look for it. By the way, a fun run (or walk) is a good idea if you are suffering with depression. It changes the body's chemistry in a way that makes it incompatible with staying depressed.

Enjoyable escapes vary from person to person. We are each unique in what is pleasurable for us. For some it is listening to music or going to concerts. For others, it can be reading an uplifting book; completing a puzzle; playing a game; having dinner with friends; being together with family and enjoying each other; being out in nature for hikes or picnics; taking short or long trips to someplace new; weekend vacations; ice skating; snowshoeing; boating; etc. Whatever it is for you, place more fun in your life while you are under the distress of dealing with your crisis.

> Weeping may linger for the night, but joy comes with
> the morning.
> —Psalm 30:5b

Facing the Storms

When the storms of life show up, people often feel that they will never again be OK. It is easy to come to the conclusion that our lives have been broken in a way that we cannot recover from, that is not fixable. The storm may make us feel that it will never end, but remember that it will eventually disappear when the light of day appears. Wait expectantly for it. It will appear. Take away from the turbulence the power of being made to feel despair. We may have to endure the dark clouds for awhile, but we are not trapped in them indefinitely.

What is the best approach when you find yourself engulfed in a storm? Most people would immediately start searching for a safe and comforting shelter, or a lifeboat if it turns into a flood. God provides both shelter and lifeboats for those who request it. He may wait until we ask. If you do not ask, you may not receive. Cling to him and he will hold you above the rising waters, so you can quit being concerned or discouraged since he is there with you, regardless of the outcome.

> In the day of my trouble I call on you,
> for you will answer me.
> —Psalm 86:7

> The Lord is good,
> a stronghold in a day of trouble;
> he protects those who take refuge in him.
> —Nahum 1:7

> God is our refuge and strength,
> a very present help in trouble.
> Therefore we will not fear, though the earth should change.
> —Psalm 46:1–2a

> For he will hide me in his shelter
> in the day of trouble;
> he will conceal me under the cover of his tent.
> —Psalm 27:5

> But you do see! Indeed you note trouble and grief,
> that you may take it into your hands;
> the helpless commit themselves to you.
> —Psalm 10:14

> The Lord is a stronghold for the oppressed,
> a stronghold in times of trouble.
> And those who know your name put their trust in you,
> for you, O LORD, have not forsaken those who seek you.
> —Psalm 9:9–10

> We know that the whole creation has been groaning in labor pains until now; and not only the creation, but we ourselves.
> —Romans 8:22–23a

> For I am convinced that neither death, nor life, nor angels, nor rulers, nor things present, nor things to come, nor powers, nor height, nor depth, nor anything else in all creation, will be able to separate us from the love of God in Christ Jesus our Lord.
> —Romans 8:38–39

Many times while I was treating people for depression, we discussed that there was an approach to follow if you wanted to increase despondency. That approach is to keep your focus fixed upon yourself. People are guaranteed to reach the lowest level of depression possible when entertaining a "poor me" attitude, or focusing on themselves and everything that is going wrong in their lives.

Who wants to increase depression? What a relief it is when one learns to take the focus off of self and instead focuses on others. It releases new joy and meaning in your life despite your circumstances. Again and again we see how we actually help ourselves when we are helping others. Focusing on others increases our joy. Have I said that before?

I have always liked the song, "Make Someone Happy" written by Adolph Green, Betty Comden, and Jule Styne. I especially love the words, "Make just someone happy, and you will be happy."

I can testify that these words have been true in my life and the lives of others discussed in this book. *Several things could have brought them down, but they refused to let adversity have that much power over them.*

You show me the path of life.
In your presence there is fullness of joy;
in your right hand are pleasures forevermore.
—Psalm 16:11

A glad heart makes a cheerful countenance,
but by sorrow of heart the spirit is broken.
—Proverbs 15:13

Choose joy! It will give you much needed relief from the storms of life.

Let's close this chapter with a large Duke University study which concluded that happiness reflected in peace of mind was found in a greater measure in people who exhibited eight traits:

1. They avoid thoughts of suspicion and resentment. (Trust and forgiveness increase happiness. Nursing a grudge was a major factor in unhappiness.)
2. They don't live in negative thinking about the past. (Dwelling on past mistakes and failures decreases happiness.)
3. They cooperate with life instead of trying to run from it, not wasting time and energy fighting conditions that can't be changed. (Some conditions we can change. Dwelling on the conditions that we cannot change increases unhappiness.)
4. They stay involved in relationships with others. (Happiness was found to decrease when people become reclusive, lonely, isolated or invisible.)
5. They refuse to indulge in self-pity. (Depressed people feel entitled to receive more than they are getting. Those who recognize that nobody gets through life without some adversity are happier.)
6. They cultivate love, humor, compassion and loyalty. (Focusing on encouraging positive attributes in one's life promote happiness.)
7. They don't expect too much of themselves. (Wide gaps between their expectations and ability to meet the goals set by them

inevitably result in feelings of inadequacy and resultant unhappiness.)

8. They find something bigger than themselves to believe in. (Self-centered and egotistical people score the lowest in tests that measure happiness. Believing in and trusting God increases happiness.)

CHAPTER 3

The Power of Spiritual Healing

What is spiritual healing and how does it work?

The soul, the seat of our deepest emotions, can benefit greatly from the gifts of a vivid spiritual life and suffer when it is deprived of them.
—Thomas Moore

The human spirit will endure sickness;
but a broken spirit—who can bear?
—Proverbs 18:14

Create in me a clean heart, O God,
and put a new and right spirit within me.
—Psalm 51:10

When the Storm Seems the Darkest, Look for the Light!

Dr. Gary Small is a professor of psychiatry and the director of the UCLA Longevity Center at the Semel Institute for Neuroscience & Human

Behavior. His research, which has been supported by the National Institute of Health, has been featured in the New York Times and the Wall Street Journal. Scientific American magazine designated him one of the world's leading innovators in science and technology. Dr. Small lectures throughout the world and appears on The Today Show, Good Morning America, PBS, and CNN. He has written six books and is familiar with studies relating to scientific research on spirituality and its effect on physical and emotional health. Dr. Small also publishes the newsletter, *Mind Health Report,* which provides an excellent overview of the spiritual component of our physical and mental health.

Scientific Studies on Prayer

As covered on an NBC news report in December of 2014, Dr. Andrew Newberg of Thomas Jefferson Hospital has been studying the effects of prayer on the human brain for more than 20 years, injecting radioactive dye into subjects in order to observe the activity in the brain that occurs when they pray.

Most people who have active spiritual lives pray. Occasionally, people who do not have active spiritual lives also pray. Not surprisingly, there is an increasing body of scientific research out there about how prayer affects your brain and emotions. Many of these studies have been reported in Dr. Small's newsletter, *Mind Health Report* (among others).

One surprising result (at least to scientists) was that *prayer actually improves your physical and mental health.* Dr. Newberg has conducted scientific studies on the effects of prayer on the brain. These studies have been reported in Dr. Small's newsletter, *The Mind Health Report.* The results indicate that *prayer can reduce mental decline and memory loss! In addition, prayer has been shown to reduce stress and thereby increase resistance to disease.*

Let's look at how prayer and spiritual practices affect portions of your brain. We will start by describing the functions of each of these brain areas in a normal, non-prayer state and then describe what happens when a person is praying.

According to Dr. Newberg, the natural division of the brain into certain areas of higher thought result in a couple of areas (the frontal lobe and the anterior cingulate) being more critical for health and happiness than the rest of the brain. As you age, these areas become increasingly critical. It has been found that prayer stimulates these two parts of the brain. That answers why prayer influences your health and happiness in a measurable manner.

Over time and with age, the frontal lobe can begin to shrink. Shrinkage of the frontal lobe has been associated with memory loss, mental decline and even dementia and Alzheimer's. The good news is that *prayer stimulates the frontal lobe of the brain and that helps prevent shrinkage due to aging. It also helps people stay healthier.* That is correct—prayer not only acts in a supernatural or divine manner (calling on God to intercede in your particular circumstance), but it also acts in a natural manner (your brain is primed to produce positive outcomes when you engage in meaningful moments of prayer and meditation).

When we feel compassion or empathy for others, we are using the anterior cingulate area of the brain. In addition to stimulating your frontal lobe, prayer activates your anterior cingulate. This area of the brain is what sets us apart from lower animals. It is important in building healthy relationships with others.

This is where the brain confirms what we have been saying so far. When you respond to crisis events by doing good in other people's lives, you take your focus off of yourself and you will end up with better emotional and physical health than you would have otherwise.

Interestingly, there are two areas of the brain that we do not want to stimulate and those are the parietal lobe and the limbic system. When the parietal lobe is stimulated, it gives us a sense of being lonely and feeling isolated from others. Dr. Newberg reports that the time spent praying, attending religious services, and singing serve to deactivate the parietal lobe. We feel more connected with life and others when the parietal lobe is not overly stimulated. If you want to take your attention off of your problems, your parietal lobe is your enemy.

The interesting aspect of these studies is that, while we cannot control what each particular part of our brain does, we can control which part of the brain is being activated. Prayer flips the switch on the frontal lobe, which causes us to experience peace, a decrease in feelings of stress, and increased connectedness to those around us. Another interesting finding in Dr. Newberg's studies is that prayer reduces the experience of pain in your body because the parietal lobe is also the seat of pain.

In other studies on chronic pain, it was discovered that people who prayed or concentrated on positive thoughts were less affected by pain and had a more positive outlook on life.

If you are wondering where negative emotions like depression, anger, resentment, anxiety, fear, and a pessimistic attitude are produced, it is in the limbic system. These are primitive emotions that were developed to encourage us to escape from dangerous situations. They were important to the flight or fight reactions that were necessary for survival during the formative years of life. Prayer actually shuts off the limbic system. Today, negative emotions are rarely healthy either physically or psychologically. We want to avoid them to improve our overall quality of life. The opposite of these is peace, which is what we gain when these negative, primitive emotions are shut down.

It is one thing to experience fear when we are cornered by a tiger. It is another thing to experience it when we move into the deepest wellspring of negativity that we possess and we begin to fear events which are unlikely to ever occur. We want to avoid this kind of fear in order to improve our overall quality of life.

These studies report that short prayers of five minutes or less have no significant impact on brain activity. It is when a person is in a prayer state for longer periods that the frontal lobe and anterior cingulate are stimulated and the limbic system and parietal lobe are deactivated. All of these changes create a win/win situation for us.

In 2010, *Science Daily* reported on studies conducted at Florida State University Psychological Sciences. These studies indicated that prayer increases your capacity for forgiveness. The result of forgiveness (according to another study there) is an increase in both satisfaction with life and improvement in overall health. In other words, forgiveness is good for you, and prayer produces a fantastic pathway to forgiveness.

The *American Journal of Psychiatry* has reported that several studies indicate that *people who pray and are spiritually involved have significantly less depression* than the general population.

The *International Journal of Psychiatry in Medicine* reported on the findings of a study of 6,000 Californians between the ages of 21 and 75 who attended religious services regularly. These studies demonstrated a reduction in diseases and death similar to the reduction that is found in people who do not smoke or drink alcoholic beverages excessively.

That's right. *Going to church is as good for your health as giving up cigarettes and excessive alcohol!*

Researchers at Duke University studied 4,000 people aged 65 and older and discovered a 40% lower risk of high blood pressure existed in people who prayed daily and weekly attended religious services. Findings at Yale University School of Medicine were similar. They studied 2,000 people age 65 or older and found that those who attended religious services were less likely to become physically disabled or to lose their mental facilities.

Health Psychology reported on 42 studies covering 125,000 people, finding that those who are actively involved in spiritual practices are healthier overall and live longer. In addition, research findings from the University of Iowa indicated that *people who engage in regular spiritual practices had a higher resistance to viruses and other infections which, they concluded, accounted for their healthier and longer life span.*

In a longitudinal study, The Harvard School of Public Health followed 28,000 men between 42 and 77 years of age for 10 years. Their research findings indicated that those who had no personal friends or spiritual practices had increased risk of dying from heart conditions according to the report of this study in the *American Journal of Epidemiology.*

We could go on and on with more research findings on the tie between spirituality and health or emotional well being. These studies provide a sound basis to conclude that engaging in spiritual activities promotes a positive physical and emotional outcome in the lives of those who participate. It is clear that our minds and bodies were primed to benefit by the mere act of prayer and worship. It's remarkable the number of ways in which a healthy worship and prayer life lead to a more positive outcome in our individual lives.

We do not function in this world without the influence of our brain, yet we have the ability to engage in activities that select the part of our brain that is activated or deactivated. When we engage in prayer and worship, we not only improve our enjoyment of life (through feelings of peace and community) but also significantly improve our physiological ability to handle illness and stress. When we speak of spiritual healing, it can refer to either physical healing of a body or emotional healing when a person regains joy and peace despite the presence of adverse circumstances in their life.

There are extraordinary circumstances when healing takes place in a manner that is difficult to describe in purely scientific terms. However, it is important to understand that a continual struggle with illness is not a failure at spiritual "goodness." On an eternal stage, healing may look much different than it does on a world stage.

Remember that our lives free from pain and illness do not really begin until we enter eternal life. My mentor helped me understand spiritual healing when she told me that we often erroneously conclude that those who are favored by God will experience physical healing. Christians who do not experience physical healing are equally favored by God. God may have decided to remove them from the woes of this world by bringing them into eternal life where there is no disease or suffering.

Prayer for healing is good, but if your entire prayer life hinges on the hope of physical healing, you may walk away feeling isolated, alone, and confused. By all means, lift your requests before God! Afterwards, trust God's wisdom in how your request is best answered.

God works in both natural and supernatural ways. As it relates to health, healing works in both physiological and psychological ways. As it relates to the functioning of our brain, our minds work in both electrochemical and spiritual ways. Divisions still exist between what we can learn from observational sciences and what we sense and feel as relational and spiritual people. While these divisions sometimes cause anxiety with regards to "which is right and which is wrong," they largely point instead to the complex interweaving of spirituality and physical realities that exist in our lives.

Spontaneous Healing

Let's look at an example that can be explained either physically or spiritually. It involves the spontaneous healing of a genetic disease that a woman had since birth. Doctors were stunned when she suddenly was cured of the disease. After some tests, it was determined that a cell in the woman's body had mutated randomly into a healthy cell. That healthy cell was more successful at spreading than her unhealthy cells. Soon, all she had left were healthy cells. Did this woman win the mutation lottery, or was this an act of God? When science cannot answer a question like this, it becomes a matter of faith.

This came to the attention of the National Institute of Health because she wanted to ascertain why she had been cured. Her daughter also had the disease and was still suffering from it.

The National Institute of Health reported that she had many serious infections from childhood until she was 38 years old. After the mutation, she had no infections in the following 20 years. She was cured of the disease!

Trust in God is both a cause and a result of prayer. Prayer reduces our blood pressure. It enhances the immunological functioning of our bodies so that we are less likely to be infected and more likely to recoup when we are. It reduces heart-related diseases over a lifetime. It not only helps us to live longer, but also contributes to our happiness. God has created our body that is naturally primed to benefit from the act of prayer.

The idea of healing draws us towards God. Yet a remarkable thing happens when people of faith are not healed—their sense of love for God can be compounded. They discover that they not only continue to love God in the way they did when they were healthy, but also in a completely new way. An additional dimension to the love relationship develops which transcends rationality. Simultaneously, we discover that God is with us throughout our crisis. Discovering you are not alone is perhaps the most profound spiritual experience that a person can have.

While we will only be with God in part in this life, we can be with God in full in the next life. Many doctors have come to faith through the process of discovering the efficacy of prayer and faith in dealing with disease.

Be confident of it in your own life. Prayer may or may not heal you, but being healed is less important than being drawn into a holy relationship with God. When you trust in God no matter what, you reduce stress, anxiety, and trade off living in the parietal lobe for that of the frontal lobe. If nothing else, it is more enjoyable to spend time living in an optimistic and compassionate way than being stuck in negative and self-centered frames of mind.

The same is true of the healing of deep emotional wounds brought about by a life crisis. When suddenly and without scientific explanation, a person's deep emotional wounds are cured and he/she finds enduring peace, one cannot discount the possibility that this person experienced a spiritual healing. I have witnessed spiritual healing in others, and myself as well, several times during my lifetime.

Leaving Trauma Behind You—Moving on with Life

Corrie Ten Boom with Jamie Buckingham in the book, *Tramp for the Lord*, describes the benefits of forgiving others. Corrie and her sister were held in one of the Nazi concentration camps after it was discovered that they had been helping Jews escape from Nazi efforts to annihilate all Jews in Holland. Her sister died in the camp, but Corrie survived. She knew the guard responsible for mistreating her and the other prisoners. How could she forget him? Years later, she saw this man again.

The most natural reaction would have been to hate the man who had caused her so much pain. But Corrie had experienced spiritual healing and she knew she had to resist such an easy reaction. The former Nazi guard—a man who had wielded his power over the concentration camp with an iron fist—wound up at the mercy of Corrie's grace and she was surprised by her response to his atrocities.

> It was in a church in Munich that I saw him—a balding, heavyset man ... It was 1947 and I had come from Holland to defeated Germany with the message that God forgives ...

'When we confess our sins,' I said, 'God casts them into the deepest ocean, gone forever …'

And that's when I saw him … It came back with a rush: the huge room with its harsh overhead lights; the pathetic pile of dresses and shoes in the center of the floor; the shame of walking naked past this man …

Now he was in front of me, hand thrust out: 'A fine message, Fräulein! How good it is to know that, as you say, all our sins are at the bottom of the sea!'

And I, who had spoken so glibly of forgiveness, fumbled in my pocketbook rather than take that hand. He would not remember me, of course—how could he remember one prisoner among those thousands of women?

… 'You mentioned Ravensbruck in your talk,' he was saying, 'I was a guard there.' No, he did not remember me.

'But since that time,' he went on, 'I have become a Christian. I know that God has forgiven me for the cruel things I did there, but I would like to hear it from your lips as well. Fräulein,' again the hand came out—'will you forgive me?'

And I stood there—I whose sins had again and again to be forgiven—and could not forgive …

It could not have been many seconds that he stood there—hand held out—but to me it seemed hours as I wrestled with the most difficult thing I had ever had to do.

For I had to do it—I knew that …

Since the end of the war I had a home in Holland for victims of Nazi brutality. Those who were able to forgive their former enemies were able also to return to the outside world and rebuild their lives, no matter what the physical scars. Those who nursed their bitterness remained invalids. It was as simple and as horrible as that …

'Help!' I prayed silently. 'I can lift my hand. I can do that much. You supply the feeling.'

'I forgive you, brother!' I cried. 'With all my heart!'

For a long moment we grasped each other's hands, the former guard and the former prisoner. I had never known God's love so intensely, as I did then.
—Corrie Ten Boom with Jamie Buckingham, *Tramp for the Lord*

She told him that she forgave him. That was it. This was what she wanted to say. This was what she needed to say to him for his healing—as well as for her own healing. She had witnessed the invalids that people became when they would not accept spiritual healing through forgiving those who had hurt them. She knew she had also hurt others in different ways during her lifetime and wanted their forgiveness and God's forgiveness. She received all that when she forgave the guard.

If you look at the world, you will be distressed.
If you look within, you will be depressed.
If you look at God, you will be at rest.
—Corrie Ten Boom

That quote from Corrie Ten Boom pretty well sums up what emotional spiritual healing is and how to obtain it.

Worry is carrying tomorrow's load with today's strength—carrying two days at once. It is moving into tomorrow ahead of time. Worry does not empty tomorrow of its sorrow; it empties today of its strength.
—Corrie Ten Boom

The first to apologize is the bravest. The first to forgive is the strongest. The first to forget is the happiest.
—Unknown

"PEACE...
It does not mean to be in a place where there is no noise, trouble or hard work.
It means to be in the midst of those things and still be calm in your heart." Unknown

It is possible to feel peace when faced with a traumatic situation. It is amazing how naturally that can happen when we rely on our inner source of strength, the Spirit within us that comforts us, encourages us, and gives us a peace that passes understanding. Christians call this the Holy Spirit.

Inner peace increases your chances for needed healing. On the other hand, stress provides a fertile environment for disease to grow and thrive in. Fear is another destructive force that can result in deep emotional scars which are resistant to healing.

I sought the LORD and he answered me,
and delivered me from all my fears.
—Psalm 34:4

Have you ever stood before one of those distorted mirrors at an amusement park, the ones that make you look different than you really are? The ones that make you short or tall, wide or thin, that distort your body and face? The best way to describe fear is that it is like looking into a distorted mirror—seeing your mangled body—and believing that what you are seeing is how you really look or, worse yet, what others see when they look at you. The mirror images you are seeing of the present and the future are sometimes distorted and not the truth. It is very rare that our greatest fears are played out in the manner that we fear they may occur.

A Time for Discovery

The name of the space shuttle, "Discovery," is very applicable to people who are passing through crisis situations. It is a time of discovery for each of us. We learn something about ourselves that we never knew before. In many cases, we also uncover aspects of others that we had not experienced previously. Just like a space shuttle moving through a vast and inhospitable space to make new findings, we are soaring through new frontiers of exploring ourselves and our world as we wander through our crisis. Some of our experiences will leave us full of wonder, while other moments can feel very challenging.

When my son decided to become a pilot, we asked pilot friends to sit down with him and mentor him. One of the pilots described what being a pilot was like. The friend told him that being a pilot is hours and hours of beauty or monotony, interspersed with moments of terror.

You cannot spend much time in the natural elements without coming across moments of crisis.

Isn't that true in our lives as well? There are times in life that are awesome, other times that feel monotonous, and moments of crisis are interspersed in between. The most defining moments in our lives are not how well we respond to awesome times, but how effectively we deal with crises.

Captain "Sully" Sullenberger is not known for the pristine flying days that he had over the course of his career, but instead for his response to the moment of crisis when he crashed into the Hudson River. He was able to save all the passengers and himself because of his approach to the emergency. It occurred when a flock of geese flew into his engines and shut them down. Sullenberger was able to save many lives that day, due to a life spent studying and training for crises.

A crisis can become catastrophic if we do not come up with a good plan to bring us effectively through it. Succeeding is all about not letting the crossroad consume you in fear, but instead letting it invigorate you to come up with incredible solutions.

Succumbing to fear does not help you walk out of it—it keeps you stuck in the crisis long after it is over. Think about the invalids in Corrie Ten Boom's story. The truth is that our worst fears rarely accurately reflect what actually happens. Fear is not only a waste of precious energy, it can actually hamper your passage through the uncertain situation you are facing. You can create for yourself an unhappy future if you choose to hold on to fear as your traveling companion.

Fear is a spiritual issue that you will want to conquer early in facing your juncture.

> There is no fear in love, but perfect love casts out fear.
> —1John 4:18a

When you take the spiritual position of trusting God with what will be in your future, it is true that *perfect love casts out fear.* Trusting God with your life, trusting that his love would be by your side regardless of the challenging path you are walking on, becomes a positive force in your life. This helps you navigate the crisis and come out of it in the best possible shape.

Your spirit—your very soul—can set a course for you to follow when you find yourself in an unsettling situation. My oncologist said to me, "I don't care what anyone says, I am convinced it is the spirit of a person that determines who will be most successful at defeating cancer."

You can apply those words to any unforeseen event, "I don't care what anyone says, *I am convinced it is the Spirit of a person that determines who will be most successful at working through a crisis.*"

My oncologist wasn't saying that if someone's spirit was not right, they would cause themselves to be defeated by cancer. I know some remarkable people with amazing spiritual determination, yet cancer was victorious over their bodies. They are now in a much better place where there is no illness or death; a place of peace, love, and nothing to fear. Regardless of whether physical healing ultimately takes place, the more hopeful, positive, and spiritually connected a person is, the greater their chances of surviving and overcoming adverse circumstances in their life.

Meditation and Prayer

Scientific studies agree with the proposition that spiritual attitude has influence on both the physical and emotional well-being of medical patients. People have been studied during spiritual meditation and prayer and scientists can see significant brain changes taking place. Meditation and prayer gives the brain and body a much needed moment of rest during periods of crisis. The main thrust of the research into the impact of these activities is that the body appears to be better primed to handle the healing process as a result of meditation and prayer.

Spiritual Healing

For me, the first instance of spiritual healing took place when I was twenty months old. It was a physical healing. A young child who was playing with matches accidentally ignited my dress on fire. It burned my summer dress completely off of me.

My mother, who was a nurse, wrapped me in a blanket to extinguish the flames and brought me to the hospital. The doctors explained to her that there was no possibility I would survive. They said that no child with burns as severe as mine could possibly live.

My father traveled in his work and my mother had young children at home, including an infant, so she couldn't stay in the hospital with me. The Catholic nuns, who taught at the elementary school that my older brother attended, took it upon themselves to keep a 24/7 prayer vigil at my bedside. With little medical possibility of me surviving, I survived in the midst of intercessory prayer on my behalf.

I am a follower of Christ, and that faith gave me the hope I needed years later as I faced the very difficult understanding that cancer could cut my life short on this earth. Faith also supplied me with the courage to face the body wrenching treatments that were required to keep the cancer at bay.

> So do not worry about tomorrow, for tomorrow will bring worries of its own. Today's trouble is enough for today.
> —Matthew 6:34

Let me give you another example of what spiritual healing can look like. My husband and I were waiting for the neurologist to give us the outcome of my MRI scan of the brain. A month earlier, another MRI located a spot on my brain which doctors thought was another melanoma. I was facing radiation of the area of the brain where the spot was. I had been warned that when the spot was small like mine was, the risk was great that the spot would be missed and the radiation would damage another area of my brain. Pretty scary stuff apart from trusting God in any and every situation. I was comforted by people who were praying that the spot would be gone and no treatment would be needed.

In this case, God had a surprise in store for me. My neurologist came into the room with these words, "I have amazing news for you. Your MRI showed that the spot you had on the last MRI has totally disappeared and there were no other spots on the MRI of your brain."

My oncologist said, "Keep doing what you have been doing!"

I explained to her that I had not done anything. This was clearly the work of God. I had been spiritually healed. She agreed!

This happened twice to me. I had a spot on my brain in a prior MRI which completely disappeared in a subsequent MRI after people had prayed for me. I am touched by God's mercy and grace! I am blown away at God's provision following our darkest hours. Even if God had not healed those spots on my brain, it would have been enough for me to just know he cares about me. He is always willing to take my hand and help me face whatever challenges appear in my life. But he went beyond just being there with me—he healed me!

The next surprise I received was the one that followed my new diagnosis of Advanced Metastatic Melanoma. I have read that the median survival time for a patient receiving this diagnosis is 8 to 9 months. When the doctor told me that my particular blend of melanoma was "very aggressive," I was aware of the dire circumstances that I faced.

With the combination of exceptional medical treatment and an awesome and loving God, I have beat the odds at this writing and am still living approaching six years later. I live with uncertainty since my melanoma eventually moved to stage four, but I have been able to get the most out of these additional years because I will not let negative thoughts occupy my remaining time. I have had a great quality of life between treatments. In addition, the times I received emotional spiritual healing are too many to be counted. Ask me why I believe in spiritual healing.

I am touched by God's mercy and grace! I am blown away at God's provision following our darkest hours. I know without a doubt that God cares about me and that is enough! He is always willing to take my hand and help me face whatever challenge appears in my life. He went beyond just being there with me—he healed my body and soul!

> Hope in the LORD!
> For with the LORD there is steadfast love,
> and with him is great power to redeem.
> —Psalm 130:7

As I walked further and further into the progression of my disease, I decided to *focus with hope on the challenges of today instead of focusing on the unpredictable challenges the future might bring.* That turned out to be a really good decision.

The sad thing that happens to us and our bodies as we worry about things is that we begin to physically and emotionally react to them as if the worst thing had actually occurred. This phenomena is well known, but it persists to the point of destroying the remnant of a positive attitude in far too many people.

Engaging in unrealistic (or overly negative) fear places stressors on the body which interfere with healing. The truth of the matter (which I am repeating for strong emphasis) is that in the vast majority of the cases, the worst thing never happens.

Think of all the wasted emotional and physical energy when we panic that the worst outcome is about to occur and later discover that we were wrong.

All that wasted energy can break down the natural defenses in the body and disable it from effectively dealing with a crisis.

In short, the negative consequences of worry greatly outweigh any potential benefits. Frankly, it is hard to find even one benefit. Worry is a far inferior response than acceptance. Acceptance reflects the ability to recognize the potential for "bad" outcomes, without becoming consumed by them.

John Ortberg wrote a book called *Soul Keeping ... Caring for the Most Important Part of You*. He also produced a video based on this book. In it, he points out that our souls need caring for. We need to attend to our spirit and clear out the cobwebs and debris that may have gathered there while we were not adequately caring for it. We don't want our soul to be cluttered to the point that it is no longer useful to us. We keep our spirit healthy with daily quiet times, listening for God's voice while we are reading our Bible, and praying.

Becoming Spiritually Reconnected

If you have been spiritually connected in the past but are no longer in touch with the Spirit, this would be a great time to reconnect. The payoff to you will be great! Inviting the Holy Spirit into our hearts and lives is the most critical decision we can make. It is the solution to refocusing our lives in the midst of the crisis. It may have been years since you invited the Holy Spirit to guide your life, but now is a great time to reaffirm that invitation.

The Holy Spirit makes the good things, the blessings that we encounter in life, more wonderful. It makes our disappointments less disappointing, reducing their negative impact on us when we refocus on an eternal perspective.

I don't know what fears and emotional trauma I would have faced without my Spiritual connection. I am certain that my family, friends, and I have been blessed with added years together as we relied on something greater than ourselves to help us overcome what would otherwise have been a time of significant anxiety, fear, and depression.

For us, being Spiritual Christians has transformed a chaotic future involving disease into an incredibly peaceful time while enduring this passage. The physical pain of treatments and emotional pain of potentially saying goodby to loved ones did not disappear altogether. *With the help of the Spirit in our lives, we were able to find relief from pain in the indescribable peace that we received. We know it was God who emotionally healed us and prepared us to face this crisis of uncertainty.*

After college, our son moved to Los Angeles and lived in a beach house a block from the Pacific Ocean. He told us how soothing nature was to his soul when he was troubled. We went on a walk with him on Hermosa Beach. He pointed to the ocean and said, "See that? This is my counselor when I need rest. I just come here and the worries fade away."

Along with peace and rest can come joy when we give ourselves respite in the midst of God's beautiful creation, inviting him to join us. Look at a sunset or sunrise and take in the feast for the eyes and heart! There is so much beauty around for us to enjoy. Let your spirit soar into happy moments and peace.

A study, ("Adjusting to Uncertainty: Coping Strategies Among the Displaced After Hurricane Katrina," by Spence, Patric R, Kenneth A. Lachlan, & Jennifer M. Burke), was conducted on the coping strategies of people displaced by Hurricane Katrina in New Orleans. Researchers found that people talking about the crisis situation, staying informed about options available despite the losses, and praying, emerged as the most effective ones in reducing psychological stress during relocation. This research regarding adjustment to a natural disaster substantiates the importance of seeking spiritual help when passing through difficult times.

Through our adventure with uncertainty, we have learned to patiently yield to God's love and power. Prayer becomes a daily discipline. Stress creates a friendly environment for illness and tumor growth, so we aren't sweating the small stuff—and just about everything on this earth is small stuff to us now.

There are times when we may no longer be able to control our future as our lives begin to career out of control. There is another lens we can look through when this occurs. Perhaps our crisis is providing us the opportunity to trade in struggles for a deeper relationship with our loving God. Maybe we will yield progressively more and more of ourselves to God's patient, loving, merciful, and gracious presence. We can learn to develop a spirit of trust and hope, even when things look the darkest. This can bring us peace and calm.

> Better is the end of a thing than its beginning;
> the patient in spirit are better than than the proud in
> spirit …
> Do not say, 'Why were the former days better than these?'
> For it is not from wisdom that you ask this.
> —Ecclesiastes 7:8, 10

> For surely I know the plans I have for you, says the
> LORD, plans for your welfare and not for harm, to give
> you a future with hope. Then when you call upon me
> and come and pray to me, I will hear you. When you
> search for me, you will find me; if you seek me with all
> your heart, I will let you find me, says The LORD.
> —Jeremiah 29:11–14a

> The LORD is good,
> a stronghold in a day of trouble;
> he protects those who take refuge in him.
> —Nahum 1:7

Alcoholics Anonymous has developed 12 steps for helping people recover from addictions. These steps have been applied to many things, including healing from past emotional trauma. The first three directly apply to the spiritual healing we need when we find ourselves in a crisis of uncertainty. The first is admitting that we sometimes find ourselves powerless over the events of our lives. The second is when we come to believe that a power greater than ourselves (God) could restore us to sanity. The third is making a decision to turn our will and our lives over to the care of God. Alcoholics Anonymous sometimes uses the term, "a higher power," instead of actually saying God, but the initial founder was speaking of God.

Trust is a keyword here. Trust God to strengthen you, to help you feel hopeful about your future, and to be with you as you are walking through this life crisis. Trust him to love you through these uncertain moments in your life, regardless of the actual outcome.

I decided early on that I would not let cancer emotionally devastate me, even if it did destroy my body. I elected to make journal entries on CaringBridge, a site that was established for patients to keep friends and family updated as to the progress and interventions related to their medical issues. I made this decision because many people asked me for updates and this was the easiest way for me and my family to do that.

I have placed some of my CaringBridge comments in the appendix of this book as an insight into my particular process of dealing with crisis. I have also placed some of the responses from others reading my posts to illustrate how you can help others while helping yourself through crisis situations. You may read my CaringBridge posts at caringbridge. org/visit/karendunn if you are interested in more current updates after this book is published.

> Be strong and bold; have no fear or dread ... because it
> is the Lord your God who goes with you; he will not
> fail you or forsake you.
> —Deuteronomy 31:6

Worship Music Soothes the Soul

Music is another source of spiritual healing. I asked my family to keep praise and worship music playing in my hospital room while I was going through my treatments. I knew it would calm my spirit, providing a balm to the physical suffering that accompanied the treatments. I also expected that it would expedite the healing process.

What I did not realize was the calming and healing effect it would have on the doctors and nurses who entered my room to check on my progress. I loved it when they came into the hospital room, then paused to hear and absorb the peace and calm that came from that music. They seemed to want to hang around for awhile. I could see that it was calming to them and eased their suffering from watching some of their patients not respond to the treatment and pass away under their care. Even though I was in the heavy aftereffects of the treatments and they could witness my suffering, we gave my caretakers moments of refuge from their normal rounds through the soothing effect of the music.

This may sound like an interesting application of spiritual healing, but I keep thinking about the story of *The Little Engine That Could, written* by Watty Piper. It was a story I read to my children when they were young. Are you familiar with that story? It is about a train of Christmas toys for poor children that hadn't been delivered to them because there was no engine to lift the payload over a steep hill.

A little engine in the train yard, which was only used for coupling one car to another car, wanted very much to get the toys to the children in time for Christmas. He knew that wouldn't happen unless he did something that had never been done before. The little engine needed to do what the larger engines could do. He needed to attach himself to that long train and get the train over a tall mountain. He wasn't certain that he could do it, but he was certain that he needed to try.

As he was climbing up the mountain, pulling the toy train behind him, the little engine kept repeating a phrase. "I think I can! I think I can! I think I can!" After a lot of huffing and puffing and sheer determination, he made it over the mountain and on the way down his phrase became, "I thought I could! I thought I could! I thought I could!"

When you are facing mountains in your life caused by crises, practice saying, "I think I can! I think I can! I think I can!" Or better than that say, "With God I can! With God I can! With God I can!" Then say, "I thought we could! I thought we could! And we did!"

Decide to give yourself refuge from the storms of your life. Be a diligent soul keeper and lifter of your spirits when uncertainties would love to snuff out the most important part of you—your spirit.

> It is the Lord who goes before you. He will be with you; he will not fail you or forsake you. Do not fear or be dismayed.
> —Deuteronomy 31:8

CHAPTER 4

Quit Focusing on Problem: Focus on Solutions

No matter how big your obstacles or challenges are, God created you to find a solution to overcome them.
—Erwin McManus, Global Leadership Summit

You are the most difficult person you will ever lead.
—Bill Hybels, Global Leadership Summit

Be kind, for everyone you meet is fighting a hard battle.
—Plato

Some people are trained to immediately focus on solutions when they encounter a problem. My son has explained to me how aviators respond to crisis situations in the sky.

Although pilots operate in a time sensitive environment, it is, nonetheless, important for them to be deliberate in their decision making process. There is a certain mixture of knowledge, technique, and discipline that pilots must summon when they are faced with life-threatening scenarios. Responses to adverse flight conditions must be made in a timely (and sometimes extremely quick) manner. While those responses very rarely need to be perfect, they must at least be reflective of the best practices in the industry.

Pilots are constantly educating themselves about mistakes other pilots have made in the past in order to avoid making those mistakes themselves. The operation of large commercial aircraft is heavily regulated by federal rules and airline policies. At the end of the day, pilots are ultimately judged not on ability to inflexibly obey a set of rules, but rather by ability to transport passengers safely and reliably to their destination. Through careful research, education, and training in flight simulators, pilots learn the proven and most effective courses of action to take.

This makes them far more likely to be prepared for making a good split second decision when they face a crisis.

Our son, Stan, now performs safety audits for a major airline (to go along with his regular flying duties). His first job as a professional pilot involved flying smaller (and much older) airplanes, which regularly experienced mechanical failures. As a result of his experiences, he has developed the confidence to approach a myriad of challenging circumstances with the resolve to find the best possible outcome, despite sometimes life threatening circumstances.

One of those circumstances was related in an article that he wrote for *Flying Magazine,* during which a serious winter storm resulted in a very difficult outcome for the flight. Our son was in command of that flight. He saw a problem with a tail freeze caused by ice accumulating in flight, and he didn't stay frozen there. He had confidence something could be done to resolve the inflight problem and he went into action with probable solutions. The passengers on his flight deplaned uninjured!

Both our son, Stan, and our son-in-law, Ron, are trained pilots who have been conditioned to make split second decisions while in flight. We, on the other hand, are not trained or inclined to come up with rapid solutions, so it takes us a little more time to adjust to a situation. We wish we could make good split second decisions like Stan and Ron.

Years ago (when our children were still young), we had been vacationing in Florida and it was time to return home to Colorado. A large snowstorm had swept over the Rocky Mountain region while we were gone. We were welcomed back to not only snow packed and icy roads, but also large snowdrifts that had been left behind by the snowplows. We had not anticipated the winter storm when we selected the car to drive to the airport. We had taken a very small, rear wheel drive, convertible Fiat sports car to the airport with us, and that increased our challenge to get into the driveway. We were new to Colorado after spending the better part of our lives living in Arizona where the Fiat was never a problem.

After digging our adorable 1981 Fiat Spider out of the snow in the parking lot, we carefully proceeded to drive the thirty five miles to our house. (If you know cars, the image of this car driving through icy streets with snow piled up on the sides of the road will make you laugh!)

As we approached our home, we found a large snowdrift produced by the snowplows which blocked the entrance to our driveway. We couldn't park on the road, because there was not enough room on the street since the snowplows had cleared off only enough snow for one lane of cars to pass through.

Our first dilemma, after arriving home at one o'clock in the morning, was the decision as to whether the car could make it over the heaped-up snow at the entrance to the driveway. We decided to try a "Dukes of Hazard" run by increasing speed to plow through the snow. While they would have completed this task with ease on television, we did not! The car stopped moving forward and high-centered itself on the snow mound at the entrance to the driveway. Half of our car was in our driveway and half of it was in the road (picture in your mind our cute little Fiat Spider with its nose over the driveway and its back bumper over the street).

When you are high-centered, neither your wheels on the front nor the rear of the car are touching the ground. This makes the possibility of moving forward or backing up impossible. The only way you can move again is to remove the snow from under the car until the wheels touch the ground again. We proceeded to start digging the car out, since it would impede traffic if we did not do so.

Our crisis was needing to get to our final destination in treacherous conditions and a bad situation becoming worse when we high-centered the car. When trying to muddle through a crisis and move beyond it, it can seem that we are emotionally high-centered and frozen in one spot, unable to move forward or even backward. We may find ourselves just remaining stuck there until we go into a problem solving mode.

When we are high-centered, we can focus on the problem as long as we choose to. We remain stuck until we move attention from the problem to implementing possible solutions to begin moving forward with our lives. We remain immobile until we finally grab a shovel and approach the snowbank!

Even individuals who function at a high level in normal circumstances have the tendency to fall apart when they are tired and worn out. While travel or lack of sleep can create this condition on a physiological level, trauma creates the same effect on a psychological level. If you do not sleep enough, you will lose your ability to focus and make good decisions when a crisis occurs in your life. You won't maintain the balanced emotional outlook required in order to make beneficial decisions. Too much trauma inhibits judgement in much the same way as too little sleep.

Become a Solution Seeker

The main point here is to emphasize the importance of quickly moving in your mind from what the problem is to creatively looking for solutions—changing what you can and adjusting to what cannot be changed. People remain in the quicksand of pondering the problem and feeling increasingly overwhelmed and depressed without realizing that nothing moves forward until the focus moves off the problem onto possible solutions. If your focus is fixed on the quicksand and you keep trying to struggle in it, you will find yourself sinking deeper and deeper. It is when you take your attention *off* of the quicksand and begin *looking for ways out* of it that things begin to improve. It is then that you can regain joy and peace in your life despite uncertainty.

Brainstorming possible solutions to a crisis situation is not a simple process. It can be a very complex process. Bob Beltz is the senior pastor of Highline Community Church. He has written several books, but probably may be best known for his work on films like *The Chronicles of*

Narnia series, *Because of Winn-Dixie, Joshua, Amazing Grace*, and others. Yet, even after his great accomplishments in life, including problem solving in difficult situations like film production, he frequently insists, "We are all Bozos on the bus."

We do not automatically arrive at perfect solutions to complex situations. Great accomplishments rarely come without periods of significant struggle, and Bob knows this. We infrequently have the solutions to complex situations neatly figured out without a few missteps along the way. It takes time to come up with good approaches. We are often stumbling along while looking for workable plans which have a reasonable chance of success.

Sometimes, workable solutions do not come into focus until we have made a few mistakes along the way! We often view them as inhibiting our success, instead of being an invaluable component of it. When we face uncertain trials, errors become a transactional part of our experience. We will make mistakes. The damage is in failing to recognize them as a part of the learning process. The key to success is not perfection, but persistence.

> I have not failed 700 times; rather I have found 700
> ways in which a lightbulb is not made!
> —Thomas Edison

For a mental health therapist who is assisting people in effectively navigating through a wide variety of crises, one thing repeats itself over and over again. Most seem to be able to identify what the problem was that placed them in the crisis situation. However, after identifying the problem, they stay stuck there in their thoughts. Their thoughts are often occupied with who was responsible for the problem. They go into the blame game, then stop there.

What is surprising is that many of them are so overwhelmed by the problem that they have not yet started exploring possible solutions. They fail to move their focus off of the problem and onto possible solutions. Nothing is going to change until they do so.

They may feel hopeless and depressed because of their crisis, but have not yet taken their energy away from the problem in order to work out a solution that would lead to a peaceful future. Sometimes the solution is to merely adjust to the new realities in their life that appeared as a fallout. Other times, the answers are more active, in either attempting to directly resolve the problem or to manage the negative emotional aftereffects of the crisis.

In any case, I am emphasizing that what we want to stop doing is spending so much time just thinking about the problem. *After we identify the problem, it is time to move on and use our time and energy to begin focusing on possible solutions.* Remember that you can always choose to make your life a creative work of art despite whatever crisis you are facing—but that only comes with a solution based focus.

Many of us make New Year's resolutions about what we hope to accomplish in the coming year. However, that often does not include closely examining what we have been doing that needs to be stopped because it is not improving our current situation. This chapter will look at both what we want to start doing and what we want to stop doing to successfully make it through our current crisis situation.

Our focus is often on the things that we can actively control, the things that we can do something about. "I want to quit smoking. I want to take off weight. I want to get a better job."

What is easy to neglect are the *improvements we can make by thinking differently.* "I want to stop making negative assumptions about the attitudes of other people toward me. I want to be active in directing my thoughts in positive directions. I want to spend more time thinking about my loved ones and less time thinking about other opportunities."

Change your mind and you will change your life! Try to change your behavior without changing your thinking and you will inevitably return to behavior that you are attempting to rid yourself of.

If you want to subvert your recovery from the crisis, just do the following. When you want to recover and find enjoyment in the remainder of your life, do the opposite.

1. Doubt that emotional recovery is possible. When you don't believe it is possible, you don't plan for it and you are not likely to recover.
2. Keep your focus fixed on what is wrong in life. That will stop you from being encouraged by the good. Thinking about what remains right with your life injects hope into the crisis.
3. Fail to find ways to enjoy your life despite the uncertainty. Wallow in self-pity. If you do not recognize opportunities for pleasant breaks from grief, you will keep all your thoughts and energy fixed on the negative aspects. It helps you stay in a depressive "poor me" mindset. It high-centers your life. It paralyzes you!
4. Avoid exploring opportunities for change and improvement. If we don't plan for adapting to new realities, we will not do what is necessary to move forward.

    No matter how long you have traveled in the wrong direction, you can always turn around.
    —Unknown

    You may not control all the events that happen to you, but you can decide not to be reduced by them.
    —Maya Angelou, *Letter To My Daughter*

Help is Available

There are times in crisis situations where we simply don't know what to do. Our limited knowledge and human frailty have not equipped us for this situation. At the time in our lives when we are most in need of clear focus and direction, we often forget to ask for help.

I have a friend who was battling lung cancer and her husband just had surgery. They didn't want to inconvenience others, so they didn't ask for assistance. I offered help and they accepted it. Turns out that they were very much in need of help, but didn't ask for it because they thought it would be a burden on others. I explained that it is a blessing for most people to do good for others who are in need of assistance and suggested they give others the opportunity to do so.

Some people don't ask for help out of a sense of pride. Get over your pride! Some don't ask because they are concerned about stealing time from others. Steal their time. When you steal time graciously, you'll oftentimes be surprised how much the other person appreciates the fact that you trusted them to help you. You are not putting them out. You are giving them the opportunity to minister to you. Of course, you want to be careful not to abuse this by expecting someone to spend all their time assisting you.

Often what is needed reduces to meals, transportation, or being a good listener. Other times, we may need professional help or internet researching time when we are making the more critical decisions. We do not usually have an unlimited amount of time to decide on a course of action. We could be at a critical turning point in the crisis. Who wants to blow that opportunity by vacillating back and forth indefinitely until the chance to resolve the crisis is no longer available?

Being unsure of what to do is not an unusual situation for someone in unfamiliar territory. Chances are you were never in this exact circumstance before and it came up quickly without giving you time to do all the preplanning you needed to do in advance. Most of us have the ability to find help—someone who is available to give us clear advice when we most need it. The decision of whether to follow their advice is ours to make, based on our assessment of the probability that the solution they are proposing will work.

Sometimes people with the most troubled pasts create the most wonderful futures. It is false that a troubled past equals a troubled future. Are you going to allow your past crises to create a troubled future for you, or are you going to build, out of the wrecked remains, a beautiful work of art?

What messes us up most in crisis situations is the picture in our head of how it was "supposed to be." We can get so stuck there that we don't move forward with our creative juices in order to produce good things for our future.

We can't see clearly when we are focused on the wrong thing. It is counterproductive to spend so much time focusing on the problem instead of moving on to possible solutions.

A fixed gaze on the problem disables us with the byproduct of that choice, depression. Depression causes a person to feel stuck, impotent to find a healthy solution to pursue, hopeless when there is a clear source of hope close at hand. After identifying what the problem is, we do best when we begin active planning to brainstorm possible solutions. Becoming solution oriented is a positive and hopeful approach.

Sadly, it is true that there are some miserable people in our world. Miserable people keep their thoughts fixed on what they hate about their lives. They dwell on their disappointments. If they have been hurt by people in the past, they tend to generalize that since some people have hurt them, no one can be trusted by them.

This leads to the next step in self-absorption when they withdraw from all or most people and begin to isolate themselves. Their thoughts and actions are based on their consistent focus on everything that has gone wrong in their lives. They remain so firmly focused on their disappointments that there is no room left to acknowledge what is positive in life. They are stuck in negativism. They don't need to stay stuck! There is a way out if they choose to switch from negative thoughts to solution oriented thinking.

In contrast, happy people concentrate on what they love about their life. They have hurts and disappointments in their lives, just like miserable people, but they choose not to obsess about them. They glance at their pains and disappointments from time to time, but quickly return in their thoughts to what is positive. They have hope in tangible areas of pleasure—in relationships, community, worship, and in God.

When passing through a storm in life, happy people choose to look for a rainbow rather than keep their attention on the rain.

The problem with expectations of how things *should* be is that things do not always turn out as we planned they would. When we expect that we should live happily ever after with no rough spots in life or relationships, we are setting ourselves up for disappointment. Resentments then demobilize us when we dwell interminably on them. Depression and anger freeze us from being able to move forward. They ensure we will remain miserable until we regain the hope required to face the future with peace and serenity. It is human to find ourselves upset from time to time. It is counterproductive to allow ourselves to dwell in these emotional states day after day.

Our expectations of other people, reasonable or unreasonable, are seldom fulfilled because they are reflective of our desires and what we want from those people. When we are absorbed with ourselves, we don't take the other person's needs or hurts into consideration. An expectation about how another person should behave toward us sets them up for failure and us for disappointment and resentment when they do not conform perfectly to our expectations.

If harboring ideal expectations of someone or something is bad, it is worse when we allow ourselves to have negative expectations of a person or event. Studies of the effects of bias on the outcome of others' behavior show that what you expect to happen is something you will likely facilitate to happen. This person may have been a fantastic asset to your recovery, but you will never know it after they have been boxed out of your life.

We may come to believe that we can see into another person's soul and then interpret their motives as being hurtful or malicious, when they most likely are not. It is so easy to misjudge people or situations! We occasionally allow ourselves to become filled with resentments as we smear their reputations in our mind. What we ultimately become anxious over is our problem, not theirs. We are focusing on the wrong thing. Concentrating on a positive solution is always superior to anticipating worst case scenarios or harboring negative expectations.

Finding the Light in the Darkness

One of the things I did as a therapist to help people process the role a life crisis plays, was to have them tightly close their fingers together on one hand, then place their hand over both eyes. Next, I would ask them to report what they saw. You can do this now and note your reactions to this exercise. Some of the more popular answers were, "darkness; I can't see anything; I can only see my hand."

Next, I would instruct them to spread their fingers so the fingers did not touch each other, then put their hand over their eyes again. When I asked what they saw now, they often reported, "I still see my hand but can see other things if I look between my fingers. I see some light between my fingers. I see part of that pretty bouquet over there ..."

Finally, they would be instructed to take their hand away from their face and stretch out their arm while opening the palm of their hand toward their face so they could see it, but at arms length away from their face. When asked what they saw now, they reported, "My hand is hardly noticeable. I can see everything in the room plus my hand now."

This provided a great analogy of how important focus is when dealing with life crises. The palm of their hand was their life crisis and everything else they saw was the rest of their life. There is a big room full of interesting things that you never notice when your hand is covering your face. Your crisis did not go anywhere. Its power to overwhelm you has left when you take your hand off your eyes. If our hand is busy obstructing our view, it has no time to sculpt our future.

It is a choice to take your hand and tightly cover your eyes so all you see is the darkness of the life crisis, or to spread your fingers to peek beyond your hand so you can still see pleasant things in your life, or, even better, to extend your hand an arm's length away from your face. When you extend your hand away from your face, you are choosing to keep your focus on the positive aspects of life without ignoring your life crisis. It is still there in the palm of your hand, but by extending your hand away from your eyes, you are not giving it the power to overwhelm your life. You see the crisis that is there, but you see beauty surrounding it.

Growing Through Setting Goals

> When you have setbacks as you attempt to reach a goal,
> you are not failing … you are growing!
> —Jim Collins, author of *Good to Great*

Jim Collins encourages people to have BHAGs in their lives. BHAG: big hairy audacious goal. You do not know if you can succeed with a BHAG, but you go for it anyway, according to Collins.

How about seeing your crisis as a BHAG? The big hairy audacious goal would be to learn what you can learn that will benefit the rest of your life, but not let the crisis destroy your hopes for the future.

As we discussed earlier, pilots rapidly change their focus from problems to solutions during inflight emergency situations. If they fail to focus on how to safely journey through the crisis, the crisis will control the outcome. That is true of us—when we keep our focus on the problem, the crisis controls our life. The outcome could become catastrophic.

God loves us and has compassion for us when we have to walk through a devastating crisis. Why does it sometimes take us so long to take our focus off of ourselves and the crisis at hand? He is there to take our hand and walk with us as well as give us wise counsel if we just turn away from ourselves to him. He offers us peace through the storm and has told us that he will give us wisdom if we just ask for wisdom.

> If you, even you, had only recognized on this day the
> things that make for peace!
> —Luke 19:41

> If any of you is lacking in wisdom, ask God, who gives
> to all generously and ungrudgingly, and it will be given
> you. But ask in faith, never doubting.
> —James 1:5–6a

In short, use a solution oriented approach. Even pilots discuss possible solutions with each other in the cockpit before taking action. Find the source of the courage and strength needed to move forward with constructive suggestions. Allow yourself to be led to people who can help you brainstorm new options. Stay away from people who are trying to convince you that you will never recover.

Fortunately, there are very few crises in our lives which require instantaneous reactions. But what is true of all of us is that the decisions we make to resolve a crisis (or minimize the losses from a crisis) will likely have a profound impact on the outcome. Like a pilot, we want the best outcome possible. *The better we educate ourselves by seeking wise counsel and researching effective options, the greater the chance that we will find constructive solutions which will minimize our losses.*

Flexibility Pays Off

One of the issues we need to face when we experience a crisis is that our plan A for life may not be working. *Rarely, if ever, does plan A work all the way through one's life, even though it is clearly our first choice. We need a plan B.* In reality, life is all about how you plan for and adjust to plan B or plan C, etc. There are few situations where seeking the wise counsel of others who have faced similar situations is not superior to our coming up with new plans alone. This is where support groups can be helpful. There are many types of support groups, and some are superior while others can be counterproductive.

> *By failing to prepare, you are preparing to fail.*
> —Benjamin Franklin

Grief support groups abound in our country. When group members are offering you constructive advice on what worked for them or didn't work for them while they were in a situation similar to yours, you are looking for helpful themes to successfully adjust your approach to your problem. Jane Schulte wrote a book, *Work Smart, Not Hard.* That is your goal.

When you learn from other people's experiences in a support group, you can avoid making the same mistakes. Trying to navigate through the emotional fallout and physical challenges that accompany a crisis is much more difficult when attempting to do so alone.

On the other hand, if the support group is a "poor me" group which is not focusing on best approaches for physical and emotional healing but, instead, enjoying suffering together since they are afflicted with the same type of a misfortune, don't attend that group! This would be a counterproductive group that would not reasonably be expected to benefit you. Assuming you are looking for a positive outcome, you would want to avoid that group and find another group. Your particular crisis is bad enough without piling on the woes of an entire dysfunctional support group.

There is an old story that has been told in a number of different ways. In it, a minister asks a village chief how his relationship with God is going. The chief responded, "There are two warring dogs within me. One fights for the kingdom. The other fights for the desires of the world."

The minister asked which was winning. The chief answered, "The one that I feed."

The bottom line for all of us is this: we get to decide what thoughts we will feed and which we will starve. We can feed "poor me" and starve "hope" and the outcome of that decision is frustration, depression, hopelessness, and constant anguish. On the other hand, we can choose to feed "hope" and starve "poor me," which will come up with the antithesis of the first choice. It will result in us feeling hopeful, encouraged, peaceful, and even thankful that we can keep our focus fixed on hope, no matter how dire the outlook may be. You may not be able to change your particular life circumstance, but you can choose to live life on its most positive terms.

There is so much beauty in the world that is available to us if we will just take our attention off of the fallout from the crisis and instead put it on the wonder that remains in our world despite this turning point. Look around you and find the beauty that surrounds you. If the crisis involves the loss of a relationship, there is encouragement in the image and hope of great relationships the future holds for you. If it involves the reality of loss of life, look at the paradise that heaven holds. Look for a pleasant future to fill the hole that this uncertainty has put in your life.

> Forgetting what lies behind and straining forward to
> what lies ahead, I press on toward the goal.
> —Philippians 3:13b–14a

Much of the journey of life involves putting our past behind us, accepting our new realities in life, and having faith in what will be in our future. This crisis will eventually be behind us.

It is very interesting how often, after the crisis is over, it has lost its power over us. I recently went to a concert where Idina Menzel sang her famous song from Frozen, "Let It Go," a song written by Kristen Anderson-Lopez and Robert Lopez. I was intrigued by how well some of those words relate to what we are talking about here. Here are the portion of the lyrics from this song that describe the aftereffects of unpleasant events in life:

"It's funny how some distance
Makes everything seem small."

After the storm has passed, it is amazing how differently it looks in our rearview mirror. Can you imagine the impact this knowledge would have on you if you were looking at your current crisis through this lens? Perhaps the greatest relief that results from completely letting go of the pain and frustration is the pleasant relief that you suddenly find was surrounding you the entire time.

The tornado warning sirens went off in our neighborhood and I could see the storm cloud that had a funnel dropping down from it. Crisis time! I knew we couldn't keep completely safe in the presence of a tornado, but it was time to go to the Idina Menzel concert so we left and drove away from the funnel cloud. From a distance, it looked smaller and didn't seem so threatening to us. The storm cloud passed over our neighborhood without the funnel touching the ground and damaging anything.

Several years earlier, a tornado did touch the ground close to our neighborhood—one mile away. The huge golf ball and tennis ball size hail did damage to our roof and some windows. After we were diligent in having the roof and windows repaired, it didn't seem like such a big thing because we had a new roof and some new windows which our insurance paid for. The crisis of the hailstorm and tornado was behind us now and our house not only survived, but the appearance of our home was improved as a result of this having happened.

When we allow ourselves to grow during storms and work to repair the damage, it is possible to come out with blessings as a result. If only we could see that during the storm, it would take away the storm's emotional power over us!

Controlling Negative Thoughts

In Cognitive Behavioral Psychology, there is something called "thought stopping" and "thought substitution." Basically, thought stopping is what we would want to do when we ask ourselves a question like, "What could I possibly gain from continuing to think this way?" It is a good question to ask yourself when finding yourself pondering unproductive or even damaging concepts. When your answer is, "There is no possible gain for me," your most productive response would be to cast those images out of your mind.

So what do you fill your mind with when you empty it of negative thoughts? That is where thought substitution comes in. Substitute negative thoughts with optimistic ones, or think about more pleasant things instead. You can control what you allow to reside in your mind. You have everything to gain by doing so, and much to lose if you refuse.

> Finally, beloved, whatever is true, whatever is honorable, whatever is just, whatever is pure, whatever is pleasing, whatever is commendable, if there is any excellence and if there is anything worthy of praise, think about these things.
> —Philippians 4:8

If a toddler is fixated on doing something that is dangerous, parents often are successful in solving the dilemma by merely distracting the toddler with a safe diversion. If you find yourself becoming fixated on unsettling thoughts, distract yourself with things that promote feelings of hope and peace. Find something inviting and beneficial that distracts you from your feelings of hopelessness and pain. It is sometimes just that easy to move from discord into a positive mindset.

Let's start by throwing myths and fears aside. My starting point was turning to the Great Physician for the courage, strength, and joy that I needed to make it through this crisis. I could not expect to be joyful about the melanoma, but I adamantly wanted to stop the cancer from stealing my joy. I knew I was allowing unwanted thoughts to dwell in my mind when I could not find any evidence of hope or joy. Here is a verse that I clung to throughout my health crisis ...

> Do not be grieved, for the joy of the LORD is your strength.
> —Nehemiah 8:10b

I kept this verse on the sink I went to each morning to remind me to keep my joy despite my circumstances. This joy gives me the strength to face whatever I need to face each day. There are times that I have been facing especially challenging moments, just as you may be right now.

The Peace that Passes Understanding

When I focus on the Lord in my life, I throw fear aside and instead feel a peace that passes understanding. I find myself with the courage to face what lies ahead, when I otherwise would have little courage. The enemy within us wants us to focus on the situation and become overwhelmed by it. The antidote to that is drowning the enemy's voice by keeping our focus fixed on God and the love of family and friends. When I focus on them, I feel the comfort of their presence which results in amazing peace.

Early in my walk with cancer, my young grandson went into a gift store with me waiting for him and emerged with a shiny rock that he wanted to give me to help me with the journey ahead. It is amazing that sometimes the youngest member of the family can discern what we need most at a given time. It had "peace" written on it. Only a grandson can buy a rock and, through it, make your heart glad!

To this day, I keep it next to my sink in my dressing area to remind me each morning of my grandson's love for me and the even greater love the Rock of my life has for me. When I gaze at it, I feel peace, no matter the circumstances. Thanks for your precious encouragement, Caleb.

Lady Liberty in New York City holds the torch of freedom. It represents freedom from oppression for people who have fled from terrible circumstances. What would freedom from the fears and concerns surrounding your current crisis situation look like? Would it be entering a new adventure? Would it result in you leaving your fears and apprehension behind you as you embark on this new life journey?

Edwin Lewis Cole wrote a book, *Winners Are Not Those Who Never Fail, But Those Who Never Quit.* It takes courage to press on after things don't turn out as we had hoped.

Did you know that I am praying for you? I am hoping and praying for freedom for you as you work beyond this crisis situation in your life. Grow through the journey, and you will discover the rewards of your efforts when you exchange a sense of hopelessness for a life free of debilitating fear and anxiety. Dare to live enjoying the rest of your life in new ways each day, regardless of your circumstances. Never quit in your quest to become a winner who has found courageous ways to enjoy the remainder of your life.

CHAPTER 5

Hope Can be our Final Home Run Batter

I will hope continually.
—Psalm 71:14

Now hope that is seen is not hope. For who hopes for what is seen? But if we hope for what we do not see, we wait for it with patience.
—Romans 8:24–25

What happens when life becomes complicated and you are dealing with dismal news that leaves you with a cloudy future? How do you cut through the fog so you can see your way ahead? What can you do to replace a nightmare with an encouraging dream? One word answers these questions, and that word is "hope."

Be ready to make the brave decision to embrace hope. Be willing to eagerly anticipate what your life can become despite disappointment. Make the decision to come out better instead of emerging from your crisis bitter or defeated.

Living in the Present Moment

Regardless of any crisis situation, the choices we make today are very important. People who live in the present (while still planning for the future) often live content and hopeful lives. Keeping your mind focused on the negative aspects of your current problems prevents you from enjoying the positive things that remain. *This moment cannot be reclaimed again! Hope is making the best of this present moment despite the crisis.*

> *We find what we are looking for.*
> —Shane Farmer

> *You get what you create and what you allow.*
> —Dr. Henry Cloud, *Boundaries for Leaders*

If we look for the negatives in our life, we will find them and be discouraged by them. If we, instead, decide to create hope and allow it to encourage us, we will develop a positive outlook.

There is a difference between optimism and hope. Optimism is based on expecting the best results when you find yourself in a tough situation. Optimism can be shallow because things may not turn out as you expected. Optimism only survives if the crisis is resolved to your satisfaction. Hope survives even when the crisis is not resolved to your satisfaction. Hope is deep. Hope is the power of God defeating your crisis, even when your tragedy or disease still exists.

Hope acknowledges unpleasant situations. It reminds you that you are not walking through this alone and that you still have the capacity to thrive despite the challenges you face. Hope focuses on your confidence in the power and compassion of God's provision. Trusting in God is a profound expression of hope.

> There are better things ahead than any we leave behind.
> —CS Lewis in *Letters to an American Lady*

Hope is not focused on the unchangeable past. It dwells in the present and looks toward the future, reprogramming your outlook for a peaceful frame of mind. It is knowing the present and future may and likely will still hold many blessings in it. Hope looks for and embraces the positive aspects present in your life.

Live Life with Intention

Without hope, we are living a crippled life with no intention to lead a better life. The question presented to us is, "What kind of a future will you let hope create?" It seeks improvement of the situation. It knows that things can change in the future.

> I assume that I am playing with only a small percentage
> of the facts, but God knows them all.
> —Pastor Shane Farmer

Dr. Nancy Strauss for years hoped to become a doctor, and held onto that hope until she became one. In her twenties, she was diagnosed with ovarian cancer. She kept a firm hold on hope that she could survive this serious form of cancer. She underwent treatments and the cancer was successfully put into remission.

Several years later, she was faced with another cancer diagnosis—this time it was even more serious—pancreatic cancer. The oncologist told her that her chances of survival were one in a hundred. She focused on the positive fact that one in a hundred survives instead of becoming preoccupied with the negative fact that ninety nine out of one hundred succumb to cancer. She preferred to hold on to hope that she would be the one in a hundred who did survive. She explained to her doctor that she would be one of the survivors. The doctor surprised her when he said, "I believe in you."

His words to her encouraged her to hold firmly onto hope. As it turned out, she was the one in a hundred that survived! Had she not survived, her hope would have served her well by giving her a better quality of life for her remaining time on earth.

> O Lord my God, I cried to you for help, and you have
> healed me.
> —Psalm 30:2

> When you pass through the waters, I will be with you.
> —Isaiah 43:2

People have many choices when faced with difficult circumstances in their lives. One choice is to feel defeated, expect the worse, become pessimistic, and assume there will be no more joy in life.

The opposite of that is to have hope that circumstances can change. Life can still be full despite unpleasant circumstances. This choice leaves us uplifted instead of depressed. It leaves us still engaged in the remainder of our lives instead of disengaged. It encourages us to quit focusing on the problem and begin working toward the solution. It results in the most positive outcome given our adverse condition.

> In my own life I've found it to be true that *when I hold*
> *on to the wrong things, the wrong things hold on to me.*
> —Emily P. Freeman, *Simply Tuesday*

Dare to live above your unfortunate circumstances by changing your emotional reaction to them. Failing to do so leads to an agonizing increase in suffering. Make the choice to hold firmly to hope and find calm amidst the storm. If you are not happy with your life because of the choices you are making, start making different choices!

Substitute Hope for Fear

The fear of the unknown may be overwhelming and difficult to bear. Overcoming any situation is not facilitated by allowing the emotion of fear to occupy your thoughts. You will discover things about yourself that you never knew before this crisis occurred. Some of what you learn about yourself will be pleasing. Other information you gain about yourself will provide a challenge—albeit an achievable challenge—to change a newly discovered area for improvement in your life. *Doubt and fear can paralyze you if you let it. Fear will increase your suffering, so it is not a constructive approach to dealing with uncertainty.*

Fear is an emotion that we will experience from time to time when walking through a crisis. Fear of the final outcome of the crisis, however, is the opposite of hope.

Fear helps us in fight-or-flight situations when the crisis is a bear approaching us with a hungry look on his face. It tells us to get out of harm's way. This response accomplishes remarkable things when it is applied to situations where imminent risk to life exists, but over the long term it produces debilitating attitudes that not only reduce our enjoyment of life, but prime us to fail at achieving a better future. After the immediate threat recedes, we need to stare fear straight in the face and say, "I am going to replace you with hope."

We handle crisis situations best when we only allow fear to occupy brief periods (hours, not days) in our lives. Anxiety stops us from getting anywhere in the midst of the crisis when allowed to elevate to the point that we become paralyzed by it. We can and must stop fear from overtaking our thoughts and we cannot allow it to keep us from moving forward.

Let's be clear here. We all struggle with fear from time to time. What is the key to conquering it? The first key is just that—struggle with the fear—don't give into it. Don't let it win. Another key is to surround yourself with people who have experienced the crisis you are now encountering. Choose people who have successfully resolved problem situations in their lives. This will demonstrate to you that a positive outcome can come about, regardless of how dire the situation seems.

No matter how afraid you have been, keep putting one foot in front of another as you keep hope fully in your vision as your goal. Remember to replace fear with hope.

> There is no fear in love, but perfect love casts out fear.
> —1John 4:18

> *We are not victims of our emotions. Our emotions are*
> *victims of our thinking.*
> —Shane Farmer

We have control over what we allow our minds to be occupied with. Many times, negative emotions arise as a result of what we have allowed ourselves to keep thinking. I love the realization that we are not victims of our emotions. We are the doorkeepers of what thoughts we allow to reside in our minds, and which thoughts we cast out.

Keep Your Eye on the Prize! Grow Hope!

Growing hope improves performance. Once, when our young son was on a swim team, it was time for citywide competition. We had a conversation with him, telling him that before we could accomplish something great, we needed to see ourselves accomplishing it in our mind. Something clicked for him that day. He was able to visualize himself succeeding. In the backstroke—not one of his strengths up to that point—he not only qualified to be in the finals but he was the fastest in the heat.

His swim coach came up to me and said, "I didn't know he could do this."

Well, he could! His goal was to keep his vision of hope before him in each stroke he took. All he needed to do was to see himself succeeding in his mind and his body would follow-through. Gifted athletes understand this concept.

If a person wants to have the best possible outcome of any challenging situation they experience, they would do well to let their minds dwell on a positive outcome and then play out that goal with their life. Be hopeful—you have everything to gain and little to lose by choosing that path.

When people are trying to steal your hope, remember that human knowledge is limited and God knows more than your discouraging advisors do. When they tell you that your situation is hopeless, remember that their wisdom can be incorrect when measured against the final outcome. Choose hope over defeat.

> And you will have confidence, because there is hope.
> —Job 11:18

> Hope deferred makes the heart sick,
> but a desire fulfilled is a tree of life.
> —Proverbs 13:12

> For surely I know the plans I have for you, says the LORD, plans for your welfare and not for harm, to give you a future with hope.
> —Jeremiah 29:11

God knows how he is going to use every experience in your life—the pleasurable experiences and the unpleasant. We don't need to know in advance how he is going to use our experiences to ultimately bless us. Remember this, and then trust him in every situation.

Trusting him in times of catastrophe—as well as in times of blessing—ensures that you will experience the peace that passes understanding.

Trusting that he constantly works for our welfare gives us hope. A person without faith often responds with hopelessness. We reject hopelessness and firmly cling to hope!

Think Positive Thoughts

Let's look back at the cognitive behavioral approach called "thought stopping" and "thought substitution." Stop thinking, "This is hopeless!" Substitute the thought,

> Where there is life, there is hope!
> — Publius Terentius Afer, *Heauton Timorumenos* (*The Self-Tormentor*)

Stopping negative thoughts works best when one substitutes a more positive concept and concentrates on it fully. Positive cognitions make you feel hopeful. Negative ones make you feel hopeless. It is a choice— would you rather feel hopeful or hopeless? Whether you recognize it or not, you *are* making a choice every time you allow your thoughts to go into negative thinking. Take the initiative to move into a hopeful frame of mind.

When we assume the worst is about to happen, we exhaust ourselves by experiencing the intense emotions we would feel if it did. Then when it doesn't happen, we find that we have wasted precious moments in our lives in deep grief because, as it turns out, there was nothing to grieve. I will repeat again here that you have everything to gain by not expecting the worst outcome to actually occur, because it may not.

Living with uncertainty has limited power over me. Cancer can damage my body, but I will not let it destroy my spirit!

There is a poem that I love by *Dr. Robert L. Lynn*. It is titled *What Cancer Cannot Do*. We give our crisis more power than it is due. As Dr. Lynn points out: it can't destroy hope, peace or eternal life.

What it said about cancer is true of any crisis you may find yourself in now. Your dilemma cannot do anything listed above as long as you do not give it permission to do so. That is the key—giving or withholding permission.

> Success is not final,
> Failure is not fatal,
> *It is the courage to continue that counts.*
> —Unknown (Although often attributed to Winston Churchill)

We live a life where many miracles take place when you least expect them. I have had doctors tell me that more healing takes place with positive thinkers—people with hopeful spirits—than with people who adopt a hopeless outlook. One of my doctors told me that he thought it was my positive spirit that was responsible for my making it through advanced metastatic melanoma for so many years against almost impossible odds. I agreed with him, and informed him that the spirit which was responsible for my longevity and hope was the Holy Spirit.

Although my prognosis was very poor, the skill and knowledge of my doctors maximized my survivability. I owe my doctors a great deal of gratitude, but owe God the credit for leading me to those doctors and MD Anderson Cancer Center. God gives us the ingenuity to combat disease and uses both those who believe in him and those who don't in order to heal. God is the great healer, but (as with many things) he gives humanity a seat at the table.

> May your God, whom you faithfully serve, deliver you!
> —Daniel 6:16b

What a powerful verse of hope this is. It is my prayer for you as you pass through adversity. Did you know that I am praying that prayer for everyone who is reading this book? For me, it encouraged me that, regardless of the outcome, my God would deliver me by one means or another. Either he would release me by moving me into eternal life with him, or he would deliver me from the cancer and give me a few more years with my loved ones.

In my viewpoint, both cases are a win-win. However, to be clear, I have been rooting very hard for the second option. It is not my desire to leave the earth quite yet. I love my ministry here to family and friends as well as to people who are walking through rough passages in their lives. Moving into eternity with Christ is definitely something to look forward to—a place without death, pain, tears, hurt, or mourning—just eternal joy in His presence.

The apostle Paul states my position very well when he said:

> For to me, living is Christ and dying is gain. If I am to live in the flesh, that means fruitful labor for me; and I do not know which I prefer. I am hard pressed between the two: my desire is to depart and be with Christ, for that is far better; but to remain in the flesh is more necessary for you.
> —Philippians 1:21–25

Dumping Distress

Hope means knowing that something better is in store for us. Even when living through a great crisis, Christ is watching compassionately, ready to comfort us through the storm. When our hope is in Christ and what he has to offer us in his perfect wisdom, we will not be disappointed. That can relieve the sense of distress that we feel.

In the Bible (as in other literature) when statements are repeated again and again, it indicates the emphasis of an important idea. Let's look at something that is repeated four times in Psalm 107 (an idea that forms the central thread of the Jewish Tanakh and Christian Old Testament).

> Then they cried to the Lord in their trouble,
> and he delivered them from their distress.
> —Psalm 107:6

> I Ie saved thcm from their distress.
> —Psalm 107:13b,

> He saved them from their distress.
> —Psalm 107:19b

> He brought them out from their distress.
> —Psalm 107:28b

Even when the situation may not be resolved in the way we would prefer for it to be, a great resolution for us would be to have our healer remove our distress. A crisis loses its power over us when we refuse to be distressed over it.

> As he came near and saw the city, he wept over it,
> saying, 'If you, even you, had only recognized on this
> day the things that make for peace!'
> —Luke 19:41–42

Does it encourage you and give you hope to know that Christ weeps over our distress? He wants us to know the peace he offers to us. It is the peace that truly passes understanding. It is the peace that comes not only when a crisis is resolved, but it can appear in the midst of a situation that hasn't been resolved. All you need to do is invite peace and Christ into that situation. If you want to find peace, take your focus off of the crisis and put it instead on your source of hope—on Christ, his love, compassion, and provision for you.

> We are afflicted in every way, but not crushed; perplexed,
> but not driven to despair; persecuted, but not forsaken;
> struck down but not destroyed.
> —2Corinthians 4:8–9

Love's Transforming Power

All of the above responses mentioned in these verses come about when we adamantly cling to hope! It is based on the mutual love of our Creator for us and our love for him. It is also facilitated by love from others and our love for them. Love is the key to the trust that results in hope.

> If I speak in the tongues of mortals and of angels, but do not have love, I am a noisy gong or a clanging cymbal. And if I have prophetic powers, and understand all mysteries and all knowledge, and if I have all faith, so as to remove mountains, but do not have love, I am nothing. If I give away all my possessions, and if I hand over my body so that I may boast, but do not have love, I am nothing ....
>
> Love is patient; love is kind; love is not envious or boastful or arrogant or rude. It does not insist on its own way; it is not irritable or resentful; it does not rejoice in wrongdoing, but rejoices in the truth. It bears all things, believes all things, hopes all things, endures all things.
>
> Love never ends.
> —1Corinthians 13:1–2, 4–8

These are amazing verses. It tells us that when the end of our time on this earth draws near, the one thing we can bring into eternity with us is love. We can't bring hopelessness or despair or fear or material goods with us—and we are thankful for that. It further tells us that we will be surrounded by loving and compassionate people devoted to doing the will of God. We will be receiving what we hoped for throughout our lifetimes. This is the greatest image of paradise that we can imagine and the entirety of our hope and faith is centered on it.

I know that God has brought about healing in my body time after time. I am grateful for everyone who has been so faithfully praying for me and my family. I am thankful for my amazing doctors and the medical team who are working so diligently to bring me into remission. I am touched that God prepared me for this journey with uncertainty. I choose to be filled with the hope and peace of God, whether I live many more years or leave this earth shortly. I will be immeasurably better off if I live in the present, in the hope of my Savior, and that is what I intend to do!

The bottom line here is that we can choose to use our minds for positive and hopeful thoughts that build us up, or can clutter our minds with hopelessness and depression which bring us down. Which way do you want to use your mind during a time of life crisis? I choose to keep my mind focused on those things that encourage me and give me hope. I choose to _not_ make a bad situation worse by allowing my mind to wander into nonproductive, discouraging thoughts.

Take an inventory of your thoughts. If you are angry, depressed, or hurt, what have you been thinking about? If you are feeling hopeless, what have you been concentrating on? Do not allow thoughts that lead to hopelessness to take residence in your mind!

There is a simple solution here—only allow thoughts to take up residence in your mind that are beneficial to you. Close the door to destructive thoughts and do not allow them to enter or reside there.

> Do not be conformed to this world, but be transformed
> by the renewing of your minds.
> —Romans 12:2a

Living with Intention Revisited

We have discussed living with intention, but it bears repeating here. Michael Hyatt is the founder and CEO of Intentional Leadership, and the New York Times Bestselling Author of *Platform: Get Noticed in a*

Noisy World. Michael writes about leadership and integrity. Living with intention can be very powerful words to a person who is caught in the perfect storm of a crisis. Those who purposefully navigate get the reward of successfully reaching the other side.

Just as runners strain their bodies in a race in order to pass the finish line, people in crisis, who are approaching the dilemma with intentionality, strain their minds as well as their bodies with the goal of making it successfully to the finish line.

Let's talk more about intentionality. If we take the stance that we are just caught up in one of life's storms and allow it to toss us about haphazardly, we are not approaching this crisis with intentionality. The opposite approach is taking the time to plan for how to cope with the storm while minimizing damage. That is our goal—to make it to the finish line with the least possible damage.

Hope fits into the category of intentionality as well. When we intentionally choose to insert hope into our crisis situation, the results can be astounding.

Depression can be termed "an emotional fog" and this makes an interesting correlation. A fog does not cover all of the earth at the same time. It just resides over relatively small areas. If you wait for it to lift, you may be stuck there for a rather long period. You will have done nothing to improve your visibility—you will have simply let the conditions around you determine the view. This is in contrast to you deciding to keep moving until you walk out of it. That can be by far the quickest route to emerge from the cloud. Keep moving forward a step at a time. You will find the finish line more quickly with that degree of intentionality.

> You don't usually drift to a place that you want to go,
> so you usually drift to places you don't want to be!
> There are people who just drift and they are like a cork

on a stream. They go wherever the stream goes and they end up at really bad destinations. There are other people who are so driven that they make themselves go somewhere, often through unconscious forces. That is where workaholism and other bad behaviors come from. But there are few people who live a designed life that decide they want the things that happen to them to be by design. We know we can't control everything but we can control a whole lot more than we think we can if we are intentional. The thing that we have to decide is whether we are just going to drift through life or be driven by unconscious forces or if we are going to design a life where we can really have the impact on the outcome.

—Michael Hyatt, *Platform: Get Noticed in a Noisy World*

Learned Helplessness

Martin Seligman was a researcher in human behavior. He studied a concept called "learned helplessness." Learned helplessness can become a pattern of responding when a person is repeatedly subjected to an adverse stimulus (like repeatedly receiving an electric shock) that he or she cannot escape from. Eventually, people stop trying to avoid the stimulus and begin to behave as if they are utterly helpless to change the situation (they keep accepting the electric shock). When opportunities to escape are available, this trait will inhibit the person from actually taking any action to resolve it. The person has become conditioned to believe that the situation is beyond any ability to change, so there is no attempt to influence the outcome.

When a person is stuck in "learned helplessness," they become passive observers of their life. They assume they have no control over problems. They also believe they have no control over where their mind drifts to, even if it is drifting into self-destructive behaviors. In short, they are convinced that they cannot exercise any influence over the life crisis that they are facing.

There is an interesting fact about learned helplessness. Helplessness is a lie that some people have come to believe because of the damaging effects of past crises. It is an appealing lie for people who have had hopes dashed in other crises, because it appears to be very pragmatic. Why double your disappointment in the end by hoping that something more positive will occur instead?

The problem with helplessness is that it is a nuclear response to a minor error. Do not ignore (or fail to prepare) for a realistic negative outcome, but do not become consumed by it as though it is a foregone conclusion.

Keep striving to better your condition and never fail to recognize that the one place where you can always improve your state is modifying your outlook to one of hope. This hope is not always (or even predominantly) that you will be cured or that the crisis will go away. With some action on your part, you will eventually enter a place of peace. This moment of crisis lasts only a little while. With anticipation of eternity, the temporary stabs of pain lose their ability to devastate your emotional outlook.

The truth is that we are not helpless beings. We can have great influence over moving toward positive outcomes and hopefulness versus just drifting toward adverse outcomes and hopelessness. *Learned helplessness almost guarantees a negative outcome.* Do you want to follow that direction, or do you want to begin to direct your life and have some influence over the outcome of your crisis?

Get clear on what you want out of life when this crisis has passed. If you get clear on what you want, then the resources and knowledge of how to move forward will be successfully applied by you. Hope is always available to help you cope with any adverse situation.

An antidote to feelings of hopelessness is an attitude of gratitude. Regardless of what crisis is planted in our lives, there are many things remaining that we can acknowledge and feel thankful for. When we notice what is positive in our lives, we take our attention away from what is hurting us and turn it to the hope that a thankful heart leads us to. That lifts our spirits and equips us to face the challenges in our lives. It gives us a reason to smile despite the pain. It says, "I will not yield to hopelessness and despair. I choose the hope that comes from a thankful heart."

> Suffering produces endurance, and endurance produces character, and character produces hope, and hope does not disappoint us, because God's love has been poured into our hearts through the Holy Spirit that has been given to us.
> —Romans 5:3b–5

> May the God of hope fill you with all joy and peace in believing, so that you may abound in hope by the power of the Holy Spirit.
> —Romans 15:13

CHAPTER 6

Keeping a Sense of Humor

How many mental health therapists does it take to change a light bulb? One, but the light bulb needs to want to be changed.

Look at these faces! They are faces radiating pure joy. No one needs to teach a child how to have a sense of humor.

It is naturally built into most children. They look for ways to have fun. They don't need special toys or props because their imaginations come into play best when their choices of playthings are limited. So, if you were equipped early in your life with a sense of humor and ability to search for and have fun, where is that talent now when you need it most?

A child can pass through the same type of a crisis that an adult is passing through, but the child often spontaneously retains their sense of humor and desire to have fun. All too often, the adult has a tendency to feel defeated by uncertainty. A child does not worry as much about the long term consequences of their problems. Perhaps it is because the adults do all the worrying for them. More likely, it is due to the natural tendency for kids to live much more in the moment than their parents do. We can learn a great deal from children about retaining our sense of humor and imaginative wonder throughout a crisis situation.

Every adult has a child hiding somewhere in their memory. After all, we were all children once. A crisis situation is a good time to ask that child to come out and play. The child inside you is easily distracted from serious situations by the desire to go out and just have fun. Allow yourself to be distracted occasionally each day after you have been interacting with the difficult uncertainties in your life. Your crisis is a serious situation and you deserve a break from it from time to time. This is where holding onto a sense of humor comes into play.

Another difference between a child and adult is that the child does not worry as much about the long term impact of a crisis. Now that would be a change if, as adults, we quit spending so much time trying to predict the future impact of our unsettling situation. Our predictions are futile anyway. They are very often wrong as we have the tendency to dwell on the future beyond what is needed for planning purposes. It is a waste of precious time to attempt those types of forecasts. Many times they express our fears and all they accomplish is stealing hope from us.

When I came to grips with the seriousness of my melanoma diagnosis, I went Christmas shopping for my family early, just in case the cancer would prevent me from doing it later. I planned for a realistic outcome (that the cancer might get the best of my body) but I didn't dwell on that. To the contrary, I enjoyed shopping for my loved ones. While I was planning for a possible realistic outcome, I refused to dwell on it. The kid in me didn't care why she was shopping. She was just having fun doing it. Also, the kid in me could not see any reason why my melanoma couldn't be beaten into submission, and neither could I.

To a child, a crisis is just a point in time that the child has to deal with. To an adult, it can feel more like an adjustment in the course of life that will have impact on the remainder of the adult's existence. The child takes the crisis in stride and is already planning what fun thing to do when it is over. The adult has forgotten how transitory most unpleasant situations are and, even worse, has become caught up in the negative aspects of the situation and doesn't bother thinking of what pleasant things may lay ahead.

Have a conversation with your child. Ask your child inside you to show you again how not to overreact to a crisis situation. Ask to be shown how to have fun again. Plan something pleasurable to do after the crisis is over and plan activities each day that tickle you.

In our world today, many people have an attitude of entitlement which works against their peace and contentment in a crisis situation. An attitude of entitlement decreases our sense of humor and happiness in life, because it focuses on what we don't have that we think we deserve to have. This very well may be the chief cause for divorce and alienated relationships in our world.

Attitude of Gratitude

Everything changes when we choose to have an attitude of gratitude for the wonderful things still in our life. To remind my husband and me of this, I have a coffee mug that says "attitude of gratitude." Why a coffee cup? The first treat of the morning is often a cup of coffee. We want to remind ourselves when we start our day to focus on what we are thankful for. It could be a sunrise or a sunset, family members and friends, or any beneficial thing which brings us pleasure.

We have dear friends who are estranged from their daughter because she has an attitude of entitlement. She is rejecting any contact with her parents and not allowing them any contact with their grandchildren. She is an adult who is not looking within herself for why she is miserable at this point in her life. Instead, she is looking for someone to blame. In her case, she has chosen her parents to blame for the choices she is now making as an adult. There is little hope that she will change what she needs to change in her life as long as she maintains the helpless stance of being miserable because of others.

Regardless of choices the people outside of ourselves are making, we often become miserable not because of them, but instead because of what is going on within ourselves. The daughter has allowed her attitude of entitlement to lead her into very heavy drug use, which makes her more miserable day by day. For most parents, there is nothing more painful in their life than watching their child suffer.

Our friends are heartbroken because they love their daughter and desire a loving relationship with her but she is not allowing that to happen. If they allowed themselves to live in an attitude of entitlement, they would be curled up on their bed, hidden from others and wallowing in self-pity and depression. They are deeply wounded, don't get me wrong about that. However, they have made a decision not to curl up in a ball and suffer about this 24/7. They have their moments of heartfelt grieving, but they keep them just moments.

They have adopted an attitude of gratitude for the friends and other child they have in their lives who treasure them. They have decided to spend most of their day focusing on what is wonderful in their lives instead of what is not going so well. They have chosen to give themselves breaks from their deep mourning and pain. They grieve the suffering their daughter is going through. Their daughter is loved deeply by them, but is rejecting contact with them. Meanwhile, they pray for their daughter and for a healed relationship with her.

The most beneficial part about their attitude of gratitude is the breaks they insert into their lives to give them relief from the suffering caused by the loss of their daughter's affection. They have people in their lives who they can cry with as they are mourning their daughter's pain and alienation, but they still surround themselves with people who have a good sense of humor.

No one is looking for humorous things about the situation between their daughter and themselves—there is nothing humorous about that. Still, there is plenty in life to enjoy. They will not deprive themselves of times of laughter, even while passing through this painful crisis. Laughter is good medicine which promotes much needed healing in situations like this one.

Laugh for Health

MD Anderson Cancer Center in Houston, Texas understands the importance of a sense of humor in healing cancer. In fact, one of the classes they offer is called, *"Laughter for Health."* The healing effects of laughing, including belly laughing, have been studied. It is well known that heavy stress breaks down the body's coping and healing mechanisms, and that laughter is a terrific stress reliever.

Back when I was training to become a mental health therapist, I told my instructors I was going to begin a new therapy called "laughter therapy." MD Anderson Cancer Center beat me to the punch—but what applies to our physical bodies also applies to our emotional bodies. We need to be responsible to bring more laughter into our lives. Yes—that is what I said. We shouldn't be waiting for others to bring humor into our lives— we are the ones who should be doing that for ourselves.

> Laughter is tangible evidence of hope.
> —Michael Jr., *Laughing on Purpose* DVD

My family and I were determined that we would not let ourselves lose our sense of humor as we walked through this battle with cancer. We would not let cancer rob us of our joy even though it was robbing me of my health. We knew we had to become strong to face the journey ahead and knew that finding relief in the midst of the chaos would be crucial for us. We took our focus off of ourselves and put it on those that we loved most. In the end, we all benefited from the choice to feel joy and enjoy a sense of humor as much needed pit stops on the journey.

I did not know that focusing on my loved ones would have an amazing payoff for me, but it did! I am convinced that it helped me pass through my crisis in the best state of mind possible as well as helping my loved ones. Those who love you are already grieving their potential loss of you or the pain that you are feeling. If you are depressed, it doubles down their grief since they now have to combine a sense of helplessness in cheering you up with the fear of loss. Being cheerful is infectious. Choose to infect those around you with cheer.

Your Crisis Does Not Define You

Making an early decision to not let the crisis define your life (and capture all your attention) is an awesome starting point. Who would want to stay stuck in negativity or sadness? Obviously, any crisis will command attention, but only you decide whether you allow it to capture *all* of your attention. When you don't want to allow it to overwhelm your thoughts, find time each day to infuse more pleasant thoughts and activities into your life.

Schedule your day. Give yourself time to think about a plan for dealing with the crisis. Stick to the start time and stop time you give yourself for this. Schedule another time for accomplishing your tasks for that day. Make an appointment with yourself to enjoy funny entertainment each day you are dealing with the crisis (Not a bad idea to do this even when you are not in a crisis situation). Minimize the time you spend with people who make you feel worse about your situation. Maximize your time with those who give you relief and hope.

Here are some ideas you can follow to succeed in bringing humor into your life:
Rent a really funny movie and watch it. Laugh out loud!

Read funny cartoons.

Purchase a joke book and read it when you need a respite.

Go to coffee or lunch with a truly hilarious person.

Google "jokes," "hilarious," "laugh out loud."

Watch an episode of funny videos or YouTube.

Go to a comedy club and enjoy stand up comedy.

Have fun at an ice skating rink, either trying to skate or watching other novices skate.

Think of family or friends who have had hilarious things happen to them.

Let's take a look at some precious people who used their sense of humor to help them navigate through their crisis situations.

My friend Doug was forced to have a lung removed after being diagnosed with lung cancer. After chemotherapy, his screens showed that he was cancer free. This period of peace was broken several months later when he had a seizure which sent him to the Emergency Room. The doctors found a malignant tumor in his brain. Obviously, that is not the news anyone wants to hear.

As we were visiting in his hospital room, a nurse came in while we and he were joking about the cancerous tumor in his brain. Most nurses have a great sense of humor, but this one did not. The nurse questioned whether this was a laughing matter—shaking her head at our laughter of what was, clearly, a very serious medical condition. We had already had our somber discussions with weeping and shock and Doug felt like it was time to move forward with humor to give some temporary relief to the unpleasant news he had received. We knew laughter was good medicine for all, and we joined in with him when he decided to name the brain tumor, "meatball."

We were not the ones who were inappropriately responding to this very serious situation. The nurse did not understand the importance of developing a sense of humor in spite of the crisis situation. Her comments were inappropriate. Humor is healing to the body and soul. She apparently didn't know that. We were just taking a brief break from the seriousness of the situation that Doug found himself in. Breaks are restorative.

Doug had some tough treatments ahead of him, and he fully understood the seriousness of the cancer invading his brain. He had been advised of treatment options and chose the one with the best prognosis for recovery. Those were all serious thoughts and serious decisions. But this was Doug. Doug stubbornly held onto his sense of humor in the midst of his present and future pain and suffering, despite the gravity of the situation. If cancer was going to take him out, he would go out laughing. He would not allow cancer to take his sense of humor away from him.

> Do not be grieved, for the joy of the LORD is your strength.
> —Nehemiah 8:10b

Develop Your Sense of Humor

People can have a tendency to take themselves too seriously. Those who have a well developed sense of humor are quite the opposite. They look at their failures and shortcomings as building blocks to move forward into shaping a more secure future. They have learned to throw away the negative parts of the crisis and bring into the future only what will benefit them. They laugh at themselves instead of criticizing themselves.

They know how to have fun and how to take much needed breaks from the stresses of life.

Ecclesiastes is a book in the Bible that is known for its great wisdom. Isn't it interesting that it reports over and over again that it is wise to find joy in our lives?

> I know that there is nothing better for them than to be happy and enjoy themselves as long as they live.
> —Ecclesiastes 3:12

> This is what I have seen to be good: it is fitting to … find enjoyment in all the toil with which one toils under the sun the few days of the life God gives us; for this is our lot …. For they will scarcely brood over the days of their lives, because God keeps them occupied with the joy of their hearts.
> —Ecclesiastes 5:18, 20

Overcoming Adversity with Joy

Here is another great example of overcoming adversity with joy. Angie is a precious person who had a full life. She enjoyed people and had many friends. She needed to move closer to her children when she had hip replacement surgery and began losing her balance and falling. It was very frustrating to her and she was doing her best to be careful to avoid falls. She started using a walker, but still found herself falling. She not only needed to adjust to a new city far from her lifelong friends, but she found herself needing to adjust to some pretty significant physical changes.

Her doctor referred her to a neurologist who performed testing screens on her and found that her loss of balance and falling were not related to the hip replacement. She was diagnosed with a degenerative condition, CBD: corticobasal degeneration. CBD is a rare neurodegenerative brain disease that has no known cause, treatment or cure. It affects nerve cells that control walking, balance, mobility, vision, speech, and swallowing. It begins on one side of the brain and body and gradually, over time, moves to the other side of the brain and body. It is in the family of Parkinson's Disease. Yet, even with this news (and with a poor prognosis), Angie adamantly held on to her joy and sense of humor. She was losing body functions but was not allowing that to take away her cheerful personality.

Her balance problems were neurological and could not be reversed. One side of her brain and the corresponding side of her body were no longer communicating properly with each other, which was the cause of her falls. To complicate things further, the other side of the brain and the other side of the body would likely be affected as well. She could lose her eyesight and ability to talk as this progressed. She could ultimately end up in a mental state of dementia.

These are pretty significant quality of life changes which *could* occur in the future. How did Angie react to this situation? She wept and grieved her losses at first—a necessary step toward adjustment to physical changes that were out of her control. She quickly tired of that emotional state and employed her sense of humor to help her adjust. She found safe approaches to being able to continue to socialize and do enjoyable things that she was still able to do. She moved her focus off of what she could no longer do and placed it on what she could still do and how to safely move with this new reality in her life.

One example of her joy came when she was told that the brain degeneration was going to eventually force her into a wheelchair. She began shopping for scooters and motorized wheelchairs, seeking a way to keep her independence. Upon the completion of the testing for her suitability for those types of vehicles, she was informed that she would not have enough coordination to safely use them, so that option was ruled out.

What was her reaction to that news? Of course, she was disappointed to learn that not only would she lose her ability to walk, but also lose her ability to move around independently. She was going to have to depend on others to get from place to place. She chose not to stay in this mood of disappointment very long. She succinctly explained to family and friends the great danger to public safety that would occur if they left her at the controls of a motorized vehicle. She descriptively detailed a scene of mass hysteria that would follow from her inability to control even a three mile per hour machine. Everyone laughed at this mental picture. She decided to hire an aide to keep her company and move her around.

Angie eventually wound up in a wheelchair and, even when she was placed on hospice care because of the deterioration of her condition, she still adamantly held on to her sense of humor. Even though Angie's condition seemed bound to shorten her life, she was determined not to let it kill her laughter. Not only this, but Angie adamantly decided to maintain something like a normal life. Her caretakers told her she was the only patient in her condition that they encountered who was still attending Weight Watchers meetings! Many completely healthy people live life with much less zest than Angie.

Angie lived her life as an optimistic person. She knew that not everyone with this disease progressed to all of the possible negative outcomes and hoped she would not. Meanwhile, she found things to laugh about in the midst of her adversity. She loved to laugh about herself and her journey. Angie stubbornly refused to give up her sense of humor!

> So I commend enjoyment, for there is nothing better for people under the sun than to … enjoy themselves, for this will go with them in their toil through the days of life that God gives them under the sun.
> —Ecclesiastes 8:15

> Even those who live many years should rejoice in them all.
> —Ecclesiastes 11:8a

I have consistently found myself in debt to Biblical instruction. Despite disease and disappointment, it brings me comfort to know that the Author of Life has offered wisdom to those who listen carefully and who put into action good advice. The great advice that comes from the good Father gave me the hope and outlook to apply the lessons learned from a career as a mental health therapist to my own fight with cancer.

I have learned to live with uncertainty in my life and to do more than just merely live. I have learned that joy reduces the impact of negative situations and increases hope and enjoyment in my life. I choose joy! I am not joyful because of the challenges. I am joyful *despite* the cancer. Melanoma can bring pain into my life, but it cannot steal my joy from me.

When I reached the thirteenth month with no recurrences after my treatment for cancer, the physician assistant for my oncologist stated, *"You may be looking back on this as just a bump in your life."* And now I say to you, you may be looking back at the crisis situation you are now facing as "just a bump in the road."

People in crisis can easily fall into the trap of smothering themselves with negative thinking and developing a usually erroneous belief that life will be downhill from this point on. The problem with negative thinking is that it steals peace and joy from your life that would otherwise be there. Wouldn't you rather think positively and hopefully about your future if that could help shape a better future for you despite physical, relationship, financial, or other disappointments?

Negative thoughts can cause negative things to happen. Positive thoughts often promote positive results.

You are in control of your thoughts—they are not in control of you! Believe this truth and take control.

This is a secret that all happy, positive, joyful people have already learned. Choose to find things to be happy about, joyful about, and things that encourage you—no matter the challenging journey you find yourself on. Enjoy your sense of humor or have fun developing one.

The Bible puts it this way (amazingly wise counsel for us):

> Finally, beloved, whatever is true, whatever is honorable, whatever is just, whatever is pure, whatever is pleasing, whatever is commendable, if there is any excellence and if there is anything worthy of praise, think about these things.
> —Philippians 4:8

CHAPTER 7

Encouragement for Family and Friends

A difficult realization that I came to early in my health crisis is that I was not the only one suffering. I could clearly see family and friends suffering with me. I noticed my doctors, nurses, physical therapist, and many others grieving as well. The purpose of this chapter is to encourage those who are walking through a painful crisis with their loved ones. At MD

Anderson Cancer Center, they have a support group for family and friends which is called, "I've Got Feelings Too." I love that title! You are the ones too often forgotten in this journey.

My family was an amazing encouragement to me. My daughter and son-in-law, Michelle and Ron, and my son and daughter-in-law, Stan and Belle, dropped whatever they were doing to be by my side when I was hospitalized, as did my sweet husband, Stan. They kept a 24 hour vigil with me in my hospital room, intervened for me when I could not intervene for myself, and showered me with love and wisdom. This was no small task for them since it required all of us travel to MD Anderson Cancer Center's campus in Houston, Texas .

My grandchildren were by my side as well, both during treatment and afterwards in the hospital, in their home, or in my home. Haley melted into my side when she was around me, showing such tenderness and love for me. Karis has an affinity to not lose her sense of humor in even difficult situations, and she gave me comic relief. Hannah had lots of questions to ask which allowed me to talk about my situation (something I needed to do). Caleb brought me my "peace" rock which gave me a much desired reminder to continually pursue peace. My unborn grandchild that my son and his wife were expecting gave me encouragement to continue fighting in order to be a part of her future. Stella even gave me a "high five" from inside her mother's womb (at least that is the way I interpreted her shoving her hand against mine when I was feeling for her movement)!

Each one gave their unique gift of love to me, which I know had a tremendous impact on my healing.

Loving Others and Being Loved

Of all the interventions I received to cure my cancer, the greatest healing balm I received was being loved so greatly by family, friends, and medical practitioners. Love reduces the impact of suffering and increases hope. I had many people who wanted to do something for me and I told them they were doing the greatest thing, just by loving me. Being loved is the greatest healing balm in life!

Breakdown in relationship with certain family members and friends can occur at various points in our lives. As you are navigating through your crisis period, pray for broken or wounded relationships to be healed. The midst of a crisis is no time to dwell on relational pain. This is not what you need to navigate the storm. Concentrate on and surround yourself with the loving relationships that still exist in your life.

I will ask you a question now. What do you need to let go of in order to move forward? It may be some of these things:

- Pain resulting from relationship issues or losses.
- Alienation of loved ones.
- Lack of forgiveness from others for your past mistakes.
- Failing to forgive others for how they have hurt you.
- Not forgiving yourself for the mistakes you have made.
- A negative attitude.
- Choosing hopelessness over hopefulness.
- Feelings of helplessness.
- A lack of faith.

Focusing on others' positive contributions to your life is very important as you are trying to keep afloat. It may be the most important step in healing broken or wounded relationships. Someone needs to take the first step. If you wait for the other person to do so, it may never happen. Loving relationships are the greatest treasures in our lives which we need to nourish and foster. They are a healing balm in the midst of a crisis. Alienation from others results in hopelessness, while loving relationships result in hope, peace, and joy—even in the midst of life crises.

In this chapter, our family members recount their reaction to the news about my cancer. They relate their personal experiences in coming to grips with the diagnosis and the possibility they could lose a family member sooner than they expected!

Reaction from Husband

STRIKE ONE
The mole on the back of Karen's leg was a melanoma.

STRIKE TWO
The melanoma was deep and invasive—the type that tends to spread to other parts of the body. Prognosis for this diagnosis has traditionally

been very grim. However, a new treatment was producing encouraging results.

STRIKE THREE

Karen's blood marker was found to *not* be BRAF positive—a requirement for the encouraging new treatment, so she was not a candidate for it.

As Karen and I and our two adult children, Michelle and Stan II, sat with the oncologist at the MD Anderson Cancer Center in Houston, Texas while he went through the variety of treatments available, it became clear that Karen was in serious trouble. Success rates for recovery in her situation were in the 10–15% range with serious possible side effects for each treatment.

At this point, our lives potentially took on an entirely new direction. Karen and I had been married for over 40 years. During our marriage, I had told Karen on many occasions that I had the right to go first since I was four years older than her and women have a longer life expectancy than men by several years. This, coupled with the fact that Karen's mom had lived to the ripe old age of 98 and her dad to 94, actually made us feel that living into her 90s was the most likely scenario.

While I would claim the right to go first, half in jest, I actually had become quite adjusted to this being the most likely outcome. In fact, I was quite comfortable with that notion. The idea of having Karen or our children go before me was something I couldn't even imagine.

All of a sudden this entire scenario in my mind was turned upside down. Subsequent tests seemed to further darken the horizon. Tests determined that the melanoma had indeed spread to 21 of her 35 lymph nodes in the groin of the affected leg. We later found out that the life expectancy for melanoma patients with these indicators was less than a year.

I had assumed for over 40 years that, faced with this type of scenario, I would be a complete basket case. By this time, we had a huge number of people praying for Karen and our family. I credit this and Karen's amazing ability to deal with adversity as keeping me from totally crashing. The roller coaster was brutal at times with positive indicators, followed by yet another discouraging diagnosis and need for even more invasive treatments. Karen and I often commented on the fact that there was a peace in the midst of the storm that, without our faith, could not be explained.

It has now been over five years since this journey began and Karen is currently cancer free after the melanoma that moved her to stage four was surgically removed. This is a miracle of gigantic proportions. I am convinced that the multitude of prayers and amazing treatment at MD Anderson Cancer Center have cured my sweetheart and soul mate and am looking forward to whatever time we have left with an appreciation that is at its highest level.

Reaction from Son

On a lonely road somewhere between Springfield and Branson, it occurred to me that mom might die.

I fly airplanes and ride motorcycles for fun, so outliving mom was probably much more up in the air than I had ever allowed, but I expect both of us were hoping for it nonetheless: mom, because every parent wants their children to outlive them; me, because the type of person who is into small airplanes and fast motorcycles is not the type to think much about mortality. The call regarding cancer became a seminal moment in my life. Death was no longer an abstract concept, but stood with me face-to-face.

There had been a lead-up to the phone call that we received on that Missouri road. We already knew that the spot on her leg was malignant, but there are a number of different prognoses for such things: the obvious hope was that it would be a single deviled spot; the doctors would be able to cut it out, and we would be able to go on as though nothing had happened.

This, of course, is not how life always goes. It is not always simple, or quickly treatable, or in and out of your life before you have any time to feel violated by the unfairness of it. As it was—parked beside a lively green forest—mom received the news that it was not quickly treatable, or simple, or altogether hopeful.

Things ebb and flow when you find a suspicious looking spot on your skin. Mom had eventually made the trip to the dermatologist after a friend saw the spot and expressed concern. The doctor had immediately known it was bad news—but, of course, wanted verification in the form of a biopsy. This had been only a matter of days before our jaunt to the Ozark Mountains and, knowing that the results were due that very day, Mom had called to get them.

The doctor's assistant answered the phone and read the results to Mom, which included an evaluation that incorporated the unfortunate number "four." I say unfortunate because the number four takes you immediately to the term "Stage IV," which does a rather impressive impersonation of the final dying leg.

If you are not a doctor—and we were not—or you have not been through the cancer journey in an intimate fashion, which we had not yet been, you generally will have just enough information to get yourself into trouble. We needed only to hear the number four, and we were at Stage IV—the endgame of cancer, where the disease has spread to distant parts of the body and the prognosis generally focuses on getting your affairs in order.

It felt like a death sentence. And so we sat on the median trying to get our heads around the news. Mom (in her typical fashion) immediately went into reassurance mode. I am sure that she was experiencing every form of despondency you could imagine, but she did not want us to worry. My dad and I were having none of it, and were miserable with concern.

We finally agreed that we would wait for the call from the doctor before we drew the final curtain on the matter. So we drove to the hotel with our heads swimming. It was not long before the doctor called and explained that it was not "Stage IV," but that the test of the depth of the tumor was "category four." So much hinges on the basis of definitions. Actually the prognosis of that depth was not entirely good, but it was nonetheless a relief to us.

The next few months—really the next couple of years—were a collage of appointments, surgeries, injections, questions, and love.

I had a mom who would have no part of self-defeat or going silently into the night. She was going to continue living life, and, in some regard, live as never before. Pragmatism required her (and the rest of us) to see that the end might well be in sight; there was no use getting into a lather over it.

There are very few productive coping mechanisms for trauma and very many destructive ones. You can cast off, or ignore, or become hostile, and your trauma will either come to nothing or (more likely) make you worse. Or you can press on slanted and out of sorts until the unimportant stuff simply falls away, and you are left with an admixture of grief, hope, and love.

That said, and with regards to our particular circumstance (which involved illness), though trusting in God is the very first place to start, I see no indication that it is the only step that God expects us to make. Reading a book (such as this one) and putting sound advice into practice is important. Exercising willful hope and (depending on your circumstances) forgiveness cannot be ignored.

Become educated about your illness if you (or a loved one) are sick. Doctors are fantastic resources, but the treatment is ultimately your own. Accept advice from experts and act upon it, but be familiar with alternatives and actively attempt to make the best decision that you can, based upon expert advice and your own particular needs.

Mom's journey involved innumerable decisions, tests, doctors, and advice. Some decisions were easy, and some were quite difficult. When faced with the difficult decisions, do research and make the best decision that you can. Then, no matter what, do not look back. What-ifs are pointless, so avoid them at all cost.

And then simply love. Love God, love your spouse, love your parents and children, and love your church. Love your fellow patients, love your doctors, and love those who have harmed you. The emotional expenditure that comes with trauma allows for only one of two results: catatonic stupor or love; heaped piles of emotional mud—self-gratitude, greed, ego, desire—or peace, humility, and devotion to God. We all long for the time when trauma is put in its place and all we have is peace and life everlasting, but, for now, we have the hope in God's ultimate goodness, and that is ultimately enough.

Trauma calls for grief, it calls for anguish, it calls for regret, but you cannot let it stop there. Trauma can lead to love in last hours, or love in spite of wrongs; it can lead to hope in future glory, or it can remember joy with the expectation of God. Grieve with others, hope with others, love with others. Love in spite of wrongs, love in spite of failures, love in spite of loss, and above all, love God.

Reaction from Daughter

Went for a run earlier and was grumbling a little that it was raining, but went anyway. Shortly after I got back, the lightning show started and then hail, so now I'm glad I only had rain to deal with. It's all about perspective.

When Mom first was diagnosed with a melanoma, I remember thinking it was not a big deal. Something that needed to be tended to, but not scary. I had a misconception that the best type of cancer to have was skin cancer and the most easily treatable. But something in the way she told me caused me to do some research. After we hung up the phone, I realized how serious it could be. At that point, all we knew of was one spot, so I chose to hope that it would be contained and just need to be removed.

After she had it removed, the next set of events are a little blurry in my mind now, but I remember her needing further treatment and getting connected with MD Anderson Cancer Center. She was heading down for a procedure that was to take a few days so the kids and I were going to join her at MD Anderson to be with her for that, planning to head back home afterwards. In my understanding, it was still a Stage II, limited spot. I remember having lunch with a friend a few days before we were to leave and telling her I didn't anticipate any surprises and I wasn't really concerned about it.

Mom, Dad, and Stan arrived a day earlier than we were going to so they could be at pre-op appointments. It was during that day that I received a phone call from my brother telling me that they had just talked with a nurse and it was looking like mom may actually be at stage IV and the cancer might have spread to lymph nodes, as well as to some organs. Shortly before my mom had traveled to Houston, seven new melanomas popped up on the same leg. I had not been with Mom, Dad, and Stan in the initial confusion about the staging, so this is the first time I had considered stage IV as a possibility. I was in the middle of packing when I received that phone call and I remember the feeling of trying to adjust to news I had not at all expected. I called my husband, who wrapped things up at work quickly and then came home to help me. He worked for a missionary sending organization and his coworkers were wonderful about immediately starting to pray for us.

I remember walking around in a little bit of a mental haze. The news took so much mental energy that I could barely think straight to keep packing. Thankfully, Ron helped me finish packing and we set things in motion to leave much earlier the next day than we had planned so we could get there as soon as possible.

We drove down the next morning and I remember on that drive alternating between feeling the full heaviness of the situation and then, at other times, trusting and resting in knowing that God loved my mom far more than we could even imagine, loved each of us with that same love, and he was in control of all of the details.

We arrived in Houston in time for me to go to a couple of my mom's afternoon doctor appointments. In those appointments, we met with the oncologist and surgeon, who had more information and brought her diagnosis back down to a stage III. We were immediately relieved to find out that there was no evidence it had spread to any organs.

As we sat through many appointments in the upcoming days to determine a treatment plan, I began to learn something I had not expected. I found in myself a tendency to just try to make it until the next appointment, assuming we'd have all the information we needed to process. Of course, we never want bad news, but there is this desire to at least know one way or the other for sure.

Those appointments were a little less definitive then I had assumed they would be. The doctors were doing their best to integrate the new pieces of information they had and give us a picture of what we were looking at, but we would often walk away from appointments with some of my questions left unanswered. That was one of the hardest parts for me. I just wanted to land somewhere mentally, but it is a progressive process and one that has to be taken appointment by appointment with whatever information is available at the time.

So, I learned more about trusting God with the unknown and adjusting to what we did know for each day and trusting him with that. It reminded me of the Israelites wanting to gather the food that God put out for them (manna) for more than one day at a time, but he wouldn't allow that because he wanted them to trust in him to provide what they needed for each day. That's because he was after a relationship with them, just as he is with us. So the unknowns actually helped me stay connected to him, the source of all I needed to walk through each day's answers.

Once Mom had finished her tests and appointments and the doctors felt clear about the next step, we drove to my house near Dallas for the weekend—just to get away from the hospital for a couple days before she started treatments the next Monday. Several of my friends had gotten together, knowing what was going on, and brought a couple days worth of dinners for all of us, along with some sweet cards reassuring us they were holding us up in prayer. I was touched and encouraged by that. It helped me see the significance of not only caring for friends who are dealing with a crisis, but looking for ways you can care for family members who are also walking through the crisis.

We went back the next Monday and got Mom situated for her first treatment. I remember it was such a comfort having my kids there with me because in between watching Mom have to go through some hard treatments, we were able to, as Mom has relayed in earlier chapters, take breaks to do "normal" things and laugh together.

Besides the love, care, and prayers of family and friends during this time, I was so encouraged by the ways that God would show us that he was with us. Some of them are so obvious we would have had to be blind to miss them and others we had to keep our eyes open to watch for, but they were always there. The two that stick out to me the most are the following:

We had a family in our church with a woman about my age who was dealing with cancer and going through radiation treatments at MD Anderson Cancer Center. When I was getting ready to head down for one of Mom's treatments, a friend made the connection that our friend, Taffy, who was currently down there for a radiation treatment, was needing her husband to get down there to drive her back. He was thinking about flying because she already had a car with her and had not anticipated that she would not feel up to driving herself home from this one. It turned out that Kent was needing to get down to meet Taffy the same day that we were heading down to be with my mom at the start of her treatment, so he hopped in the car with our family and accompanied us on the four hour drive to Houston.

What I remember about that trip is knowing that God had worked the timing out to show us he was involved in the details. There was something about driving down together, knowing they were facing something similar to what we were, that was comforting. That drive started the bonds of the special friendship with them.

The other memory I have that stands out is during a very long surgery my mom had. My dad and I waited at the hospital and it was not completed until late at night. We were the last ones left in a dark, quiet waiting room when a woman came and found us. She was there with her husband who was being treated at MD Anderson Cancer Center. She had somehow made the connection that we were there. We had never met her before, but her mom was one of my mom's sister's best friends. When she found out we were there, she walked the halls until she came and found us. She and I have also remained friends since then and pray for each other often.

Those two examples were pictures to me of God making it clear to us that we were not alone. He was with us and would send people to be with us in ways we would not expect. So, what carried me through was the love of our own family, as well as the support of other family and friends, and those we even met in the process. And most of all, evidences of God's hand in the midst of it.

Reaction from Grandchildren

Our grandchildren were ages eleven, nine, seven, and five when we received the cancer diagnosis five years ago, and they have since reflected back on that time. I discussed with my family that it was important for everyone to openly discuss their fears and ask any questions on their mind. Our two older grandchildren did just that and their questions pretty much revolved around whether I would die or survive and whether I was afraid of what would happen. The younger ones had no questions in the beginning. In close physical contact, they clung to me more than usual.

My oldest granddaughter, Karis, who was eleven at the time, said she had lots of questions about my cancer. She was happy at first to hear it was a skin cancer, since she thought that was a mild and not deadly form of cancer. Later she learned that melanoma is called "the deadly skin cancer." Her following thoughts were concerns that I could die. When I asked her what advice she would now want to give any children whose family member was diagnosed with a scary medical diagnosis, she said without hesitation, "I would tell them to focus on enjoying the time they have with that family member instead of focusing on the potential loss of the relative." From the mouths of children come very wise counsel!

My nine year old granddaughter, Hannah, was very inquisitive and asked me lots of questions. Since she felt comfortable asking me the questions that arose as a result of my cancer, she adjusted rather quickly to my health crisis. Her advice to other children in her situation is "not to worry too much because worrying will start affecting your life." She said that, instead of worry, pray for the person and trust God because everything will turn out alright in the end. (She knew my worse case scenario was entry into heaven.)

Haley, my then seven year old granddaughter, was very quiet when she was around me, but would sit so close to me that I could not tell where I ended and she began. I could tell how sad she was over my cancer by her nonverbal behavior. She tells me now that she was very afraid that I was going to die and she did not want that to happen. She kept thinking about how difficult it would be for her to lose me. She said she was thinking about me, the cancer, and her possible loss of me much of the time.

Remember that a child may look like they are taking a tough life crisis in their stride, but what they look like on the outside and how they feel on the inside can vary widely.

My five year old grandson had very sad eyes when he saw me suffering. He didn't ask many questions. One time I went to their house soon after surgery and chemotherapy and when they picked me up at the airport, I was brought to the car in a wheelchair. He said nothing at that time. He did spend lots of time sitting really close beside me and having me visit with him and read to him. The next time I came to visit him without needing a wheelchair, he said, "Grandma, you were handicapped before but now you aren't handicapped any more!"

This was his way of celebrating that he had seen me in a debilitated state in the past but was so happy to see me in a rehabilitated state again. It showed me how sad he was when he witnessed my weakened condition. Remember that five year olds can absorb much more than we think they do, even when they do not verbalize it at the time.

At this writing, our grandchildren are seventeen, fifteen, twelve, eleven, and two months from birth (one is "in the oven"). They still occasionally wanted reassurance that the cancer has not recurred. My recent recurrence of cancer is still impacting them and resurfacing their concerns that they might lose me.

Family and friends are the most precious gifts we have in this life. Remember to nurture and cherish those relationships to leave a legacy of love behind you when you are no longer here. We will all be memories some day. Live your life to its fullest and do what you can to leave a pleasant memory behind.

> Honor everyone. Love the family of believers.
> —1Peter 2:17

A P P E N D I X

I am adding this appendix to this book to illustrate how we can encourage ourself and others while we are still in the crisis mode, and how precious encouragement from others is at that time. I knew how difficult it was for those who loved me to watch my suffering and endure concerns that I might not survive. I wanted to encourage them and ease their suffering, and encouraged myself in the process of doing so.

Since there were so many people requesting updates, I set up a page in CaringBridge, a free internet sight for persons encountering medical problems. I made this decision so friends and family could be informed of my current status. Some of my entries are included in this appendix. If you want to see all of my past postings, or those that were posted after the publishing of this book, you can go to <u>caringbridge.org/visit/</u> <u>karendunn</u> or my website on the back of this book where I have a blog to encourage people who are coping with loss. You are invited to join me on that site for updates and for encouragement for you.

There are some distinct themes in the comments made by family and friends on my CaringBridge page that I also include in this appendix (Those are included between parentheses). You see shock at the medical crisis, concern for family members, hope regarding the outcome, joy at good news, mourning at not so good news, spiritual encouragement, prayers for intervention from the one who could change any odds, etc. You will probably see yourself in some of the comments.

Loved ones want to be in the loop on updates when we are passing through our crisis. They don't necessarily want us to bleed all over them emotionally with negativity, but they do want to know what is going on with us. After all, they love us. How precious is that?

Here are excerpts from My CaringBridge site:

April, 2011
I went to my Denver, Colorado internist and showed him a black mole on the back of my leg calf. He expressed his grave concern and did a biopsy on the growth.

Local pathologists suspected melanoma but were not sure of the diagnosis, so they sent the biopsy to Mayo Clinic.
The Mayo Clinic pathology report diagnosed it as invasive metastatic melanoma with ulceration and mitosis (cancer cells dividing and likely sending cancer cells from my leg into my body). It has all the bad things in it that make this a life-threatening cancer. Wow—didn't expect to hear all that!

> Jesus went throughout Galilee, teaching in their synagogues and proclaiming the good news of the kingdom and curing every disease and every sickness among the people.
> —Matthew 4:23

Would be great if Jesus would just heal this one.

June, 2011
We decided to seek treatment at MD Anderson Cancer Center in Houston, Texas since this was clearly a very serious cancer. My MD Anderson Cancer Center oncological surgeon, Dr. Merrick Ross, removed a wide margin of skin surrounding where the melanoma had been and removed five sentinel lymph nodes. No melanoma was found in the surrounding tissue and lymph nodes. That was great news! I did

develop lymphedema (swelling of the leg) as a result of the loss of lymph nodes. The lymphedema may go away or may remain with me the rest of my life. I am diagnosed at stage II cancer.

> Help me, Lord God!
> —Judges 6:22b

> In my distress I called upon the LORD;
> to my God I cried for help.
> —Psalm 18:6a

July28, 2012

A local metastasis took place a few weeks ago. Seven new melanoma tumors appeared one morning in this same leg that the invasive melanoma was removed from eleven months ago. This advances me to stage III cancer.

I love and trust my God, no matter where this journey may lead me. I know He will be by my side and that will give me the strength and peace and calm to sustain me. Jesus Christ is with those who love him today, tomorrow and throughout eternity.

A friend sent this verse to me, and I am adding it to my life verses...

> I have set the LORD always before me; because he is at
> my right hand, I shall not be moved.
> —Psalm 16:8

(Comments from readers of my post: I've known three people with melanoma that has metastasized who survived for more than five years now and one for more than fifteen thus far! There is great hope! We love you and are praying for you. Thanks for keeping us posted. I am sorry to hear of this reoccurrence. You were such a blessing to me during cancer. May God grant you His peace and the willingness to rest and let others take care of YOU!)

August 5, 2012

We are in Houston now, encouraged and nourished by your calls, cards, emails, etc. There is no greater healing salve than love to prepare us for what lies ahead of us. Thank you for this beautiful preparation.

As you are praying for us, we are praying that God would richly and abundantly bless you. This is giving me ample opportunity to exercise one of my three life verses...

> Trust in the LORD with all your heart, and do not rely
> on your own insight. In all your ways acknowledge him,
> and he will make straight your paths.
> —Proverbs 3:5–6

(Comments: Your positive attitude despite your circumstances is an inspiration to all of us. You seem so positive and why not, when you have the greatest physician of all right at your side! I also pray for Stan and your children as this isn't easy on family members either.

In our thoughts and prayers as you face this journey through the unknown.)

August 6, 2012

Today's testing verified that the melanoma has moved into my lymph nodes. That puts me in stage IIIC, the highest stage three category. MD Anderson plus Christ can perform miracles.

Thanks for your prayers. Please remember to keep my family in your prayers.

(Comments: I am so sorry to hear about this new development and increased challenge. Thank you for being so brave and trusting in your faith. So sorry to hear about this last development. Stay strong! We love you!

I'm sorry you're facing this but so comforted by the fact that you rely so heavily upon the Lord. Keep that wonderful, positive attitude going and the best is yet to come. I know this was not the information you wanted to hear but nothing is impossible for our amazing God. I am praying for His Healing Hand to be upon you and peace for your family. As I worked in my garden this morning, I was thinking and praying about you; I'm praying for you this morning, that God's peace will reign in your heart. We love you. May you be nourished, strengthened and comforted today and each day until you return home. We love you guys.)

August 7, 2012

The good news is that the brain MRI and the PET scan did not show melanoma anywhere but the right leg, so I am still at stage IIIC. After a five hour consultation with the medical team, they decided the best course of action, given the aggressive and fast moving character of the melanoma, is to use systemic bio-immuno therapy first.

It is not a chemotherapy but instead is a biological approach to wake up my immune system and encourage it to start attacking the melanomas.

The treatment approach will be my being admitted to the MD Anderson hospital and administered the bio-immuno therapy through an IV. A heart monitor will be placed on me. I will need to stay in the hospital for four days to ensure none of the bad reactions are taking place. Then I will go home for fourteen days and return for another week repeating that process. There will be four treatment rounds. There is a 40% chance that this approach will shrink the tumors at least 50%. If it doesn't work, we go to plan B. Thanks for your prayers and encouragement.

(Comments: So glad to hear some positive news, hope and pray it continues that way. It means a great deal to be included among those who care and want to share in this journey. We are so sorry you have to go through this again. Thank you for putting this Caring Bridge site together.)

June 1, 2013 3:33pm

> For I will restore health to you,
> and your wounds I will heal,
> says The LORD.
> —Jeremiah 30:17

For two years, as a result of my cancer, I have undergone eight surgical procedures, two rounds of bio-immuno therapy, and one round of intensive chemotherapy to my leg. These have resulted in considerable healing periods which have involved more than half of the time during those two years. The procedures were difficult, and the healing time after them have been extensive.

I am truly walking normally now, and was just approaching normal walking prior to the surgery. There can be no doubt that the Great Physician showed up at and following my surgery. None of this can be medically explained but can be understood when you add the One that is, the One that was and the One that is to come to the equation.

(Comments: So many answers to prayers beyond what we asked or hoped for. Well, Karen, I am shedding some tears right now, but they are happy tears!)

June 3, 2013 10:01pm

> But who can detect their errors?
> Clear me from hidden faults.
> —Psalm 19:12

The pathology reports are in. The small tumor they removed was a melanoma. The surrounding tissues were clear with no signs of melanoma in them.

June 14, 2013 7:43pm

> So you have pain now; but I will see you again, and
> your hearts will rejoice, and no one will take your joy
> from you.
> —John:16:22

Another red letter day has come into my life—for the first time in eight months, I am not starting my mornings and ending my days by placing dressings on my wounds. The stitches were taken out of my leg today and it healed well. Everything is now healed. No more need to dress anything with gauze and care for wounds!

(Comment: It has been a tough row to hoe, but thank God for His faithfulness. Your post hit me right between the eyes as I process my own current circumstances. I need to be more aware and intentional about invoking a grateful perspective. Thank you for your weekly lessons on life and what is really important.)

June 25, 2013 8:40pm

All CLEAR!!! That was the result of my PET scans and MRI today—no new melanomas were found.

> And this is the boldness we have in him, that if we ask
> anything according to his will, he hears us. And if we
> know that he hears us in whatever we ask, we know that
> we have obtained the requests made of him.
> —1John 5:14–15

August 28, 2013 11:04am

I came to Houston for a seminar on melanoma and for a PET scan. The PET scan again revealed that my leg and body are still clear—no new melanomas for over ten months now.

For I will restore health to you, and your wounds I will
heal, says the LORD.
—Jeremiah 30:17

(Comment: Now you know, even in more detail, how God was working
in your life to heal you!)

November 26, 2013 at 9:17 pm

Good news—my PET scan yesterday was all clear, showing no new
melanomas for the past 13 months! My surgeon said, "These results are
very remarkable since you had significant disease in your leg."

> You have turned my mourning into dancing;
> you have taken off my sackcloth
> and clothed me with joy,
> so that my soul may praise you and not be silent.
> O Lord my God, I will give thanks to you forever.
> —Psalm 30:11–12

(Comments: Karen your love & life continues to be an inspiration to
all. The example he has given us at HCC through your life is so tender
and touching.)

April 27, 2014 8:10 am

Still no new melanomas but another time that God stepped in and
healed me. When I went in for my scans on February 25, the PET scan
was clear but the brain MRI showed a new spot on my brain with a
bleed around it. It was not diagnosed as a melanoma, but my oncologist
said it was very likely one and scheduled a consultation for me six weeks
later with the gamma knife (radiation) department neurologist. I was
told that if the spot disappeared as the last spot on my brain did, that
future MRIs would show the bleed because bleeds destroy brain cells.

When I returned for a recheck MRI, the neurologist reporting the results of my MRI exclaimed, "I have amazing news for you!"

He told me the spot was gone and the bleed area was clear except one tiny spot where the residue of the bleed could be seen. I am certain the removal of the spot and bleed area was at God's hands. My oncologist said that my prayers and the prayers of those who were praying for me was the best explanation for what happened. If this is not evidence of God's work, I do not know what is.

> Therefore let all who are faithful offer prayer to you; at a time of distress, the rush of mighty waters shall not reach them. You are a hiding place for me; you preserve me from trouble; you surround me with glad cries of deliverance.
> —Psalm 32:6–7

June 10, 2014 11:40pm

I came to Houston for my routine scans. A few days earlier, a swollen area that looked like an insect bite appeared near where most of my previous melanomas were. My scan results showed that I have another melanoma.

A new targeted chemotherapy, which is injected directly into the tumor, was designed to destroy tumors but in clinical studies it has been shown to not only destroy the melanoma, but then to create an immune response in the body which in turn protects the body from future melanomas. My surgeon, Dr Merrick Ross at MD Anderson Cancer Center, is one of the few doctors in the nation who have been approved to give this treatment. I have been selected to receive this treatment.

> For surely I know the plans I have for you, says the LORD, plans for your welfare and not for harm, to give you a future with hope. Then when you call upon me

and come and pray to me, I will hear you. When you search for me, you will find me; if you seek me with all your heart, I will let you find me, says the LORD.
—Jeremiah 29:11–14

June 11, 2014 5:38pm

While darkness (melanomas) may be messing with my body, they are not allowed to enter my mind and I refuse to let this situation drain any joy or peace from my life. Emotionally I am doing great, although my body is giving me a run for my money. Now the challenge is to try to get the physical in line with the mental :)

I am scheduled for my clinical trial injection on the melanoma tomorrow (Thursday) at 11:45 am. It appears that Dr. Ross is giving up his lunchtime to do this. He is my hero in how much of his life he sacrifices to heal cancer in his patients.

> Peace I leave with you; my peace I give to you. I do not give to you as the world gives. Do not let your hearts be troubled, and do not let them be afraid.
> —John 14:27

June 12, 2014 10:21pm

I had my injection as planned this morning, and so far, the side effects are minimal. I am hoping this wipes out the melanoma. If not, Dr. Ross will inject it again after a month or two passes since some responses are not achieved until the second injection.

> In your book were written all the days that were formed for me, when none of them as yet existed. How weighty to me are your thoughts, O God! How vast is the sum of them! I try to count them—they are more than the sand; I come to the end—I am still with you.
> —Psalm 139:16b–18

Thanks for a good day, Lord, and for showing up to walk through this with me. Thanks also for the prayers others have lifted to you for me. Please abundantly bless them for their kindness.

July 8, 2014 1:24pm

I am going to receive another injection into my tumor today since the tumor has not disappeared yet, even though it is less dense than it was. If this doesn't get rid of the tumor within the next four weeks, my surgeon will surgically remove it. Even if the tumor is not destroyed, the injection still may create an immune response in my body that will destroy any microscopic melanoma cells that may be floating around. Another month of waiting to see if this injection succeeds in destroying the tumor...

> Those who wait for the Lord shall renew their strength,
> they shall mount up with wings like eagles, they shall
> run and not be weary, they shall walk and not faint.
> —Isaiah 40:31

(Comment: Thank you for modeling such faith and strength)

August 7, 2014 10:13pm

The good news is that my melanoma continues to shrink and there is evidence that my immune system is being stimulated to wipe out melanoma cells, so the decision was made by my surgeon to give me another injection. This injection results in my being given a full therapeutic dose, so will be my last injection. I know the one who created my immune system and who can heal any disease. I am not confused about where my help comes from.

> I am The LORD;
> in its time I will accomplish it quickly.
> —Isaiah 60:22b

September 7, 2014 7:49pm

The clinical trail was at least partially successful since it shrunk my melanoma. When I went in for my checkup last Thursday, my surgeon decided that it was time to take the melanoma out since it had not completely disappeared. It did change color, which could have indicated that the melanoma cells were destroyed in it and only scarred tissue remained.

My melanoma was surgically removed. Again, I had another miracle following the surgery. From the day after my surgery, I had no pain in my leg. It has healed well and I am able to continue normal activities only the second day after my surgery!

We have a tendency to focus on the big details. It appears that God focuses on the seemingly small details during our healing process. How is it possible that I could have no pain after the first day of this surgery as well as the previous surgery? God gave me a truly amazing surgeon, and then He personally intervened in the healing details.

> And those who know your name put their trust in you,
> for you, O LORD, have not forsaken those who seek you.
> —Psalm 9:10

September 17, 2014 9:16am

The pathology reports from the melanoma that was removed from my leg shows that the entire melanoma was removed and the surrounding tissue around the melanoma including deep tissue was clear (had no melanoma cells in it). This was certainly good news. Once again, by the grace and mercy of God, I am cancer free!

> Better is the end of a thing than its beginning;
> the patient in spirit are better than the proud in spirit...
> Do not say, 'Why were the former days better than these?'

For it is not from wisdom that you ask this.
—Ecclesiastes 7:8, 10

Hope does not disappoint us, because God has poured
out his love into our hearts.
—Romans 5:5

December 17, 2014 11:22pm

I just had routine scans at MD Anderson Cancer Center, and no cancer
was diagnosed from either my brain MRI or my PET scan. That was
awesome, but the miracles surrounding my journey with a very serious
form of cancer, advanced metastatic melanoma, continue to abound.

Your servant has found favor with you, and you have
shown me great kindness in saving my life.
—Genesis 19:19

March, 2016

I am now going in for 6 month check ups and my last check up and
scans still showed me to be cancer free. Thanks for all the prayers and
love you have so freely shown our family during and following my
cancer treatments.

Many of you have been encouraging me to write a book to help others
who are going through significant life crises, since you have told me how
helpful my postings on Caring Bridge have been to you in adjusting to
difficult life crises in your own lives. Because of your prompting, I have
been writing a book during the past three years to encourage people
who were passing through medical or other life crises. The title is *Living
With Uncertainty and Still Enjoying Life*. I am close to completing the
book and now am investigating possible publishers.

September 28, 2016

I went in to MD Anderson Cancer Center for my 6 month cancer screens yesterday. The MRI was clear. The PET scan did not result in a cancer diagnosis, but there was a suspicious area in my small intestine classified as undetermined. Dr. Ross said it could be anything, but he wants to rule out cancer. They have me scheduled for a CT scan on Friday at 2pm—best laid plans always subject to change for me ...

October 13, 2016

My medical team at MD Anderson Cancer Center are convinced the area on my small intestine is metastatic melanoma. I will meet with my surgeon, Dr. Ross, and the oncological team to discuss treatment options. Meanwhile, I will be walking in the peace that passes understanding that my Lord provides and not let it steal one bit of joy from my heart ...

> O Most High, when I am afraid,
> I put my trust in you.
> In God, whose word I praise,
> In God I trust; I am not afraid.
> —Psalm 56:2b–4

> Peace I leave with you; my peace I give to you. I do not give to you as the world gives. Do not let your hearts be troubled, and do not let them be afraid.
> —John 14:27

October 23, 2016

> At an acceptable time I have listened to you,
> and on a day of salvation I have helped you.
> —2Corinthians 6:2

I am so thankful that God provided me two and a half years of cancer free time. I hope I used it well for him. He used it well for me. My goal of writing a book to help others who are going through difficult life passages was accomplished. I wrote it together with my family and we are doing our final edits on the book now and then will send it to our publisher for their final edits. Our title is *Living With Uncertainty and Still Enjoying Life.* The subtitle is, "A Family Survival Guide for Those Whose Lives Have Been Interrupted by a Crisis." It is all about finding peace in the midst of a storm.

As expected, the lab results confirmed that the area in my small intestine is malignant metastatic melanoma and this is a bleeding melanoma. My medical team has decided to schedule surgery soon because of the blood loss issue that has occurred with me. I will be admitted to the hospital on Sunday and the surgery will take place on Monday.

> He has said, 'I will never leave you or forsake you.'
> So we can say with confidence,
> 'The Lord is my helper;
> I will not be afraid.
> What can anyone do to me?'
> —Hebrews 13:5–6

November 7, 2016

During my recent bout with small bowel cancer that moved me into Stage IV, I have learned many things. It has helped me refocus once again on all that I am thankful for. The challenges in facing the crisis of a serious disease and your mortality are many, but the blessings that remain in my life are still greater than the challenges.

I AM SO THANKFUL BECAUSE:
Christ is still in my life, no matter what I encounter on earth. He loves me unswervingly. He is my source of strength when I need strength. He is my comforter. He is my joy. He remains my first love despite any unpleasant circumstances I might find myself in.

My husband and children were by my side during the hospitalization following the surgery. Stan slept in my room each night because he wanted to be there for me.

I have received incredible love and prayers from so many precious people.

The ONLY spot that was found to be malignant metastatic melanoma was the one that was removed from my small intestine. It is rare for other malignant spots to not be found when there is a malignancy in the small intestine. The lymph nodes were clear.

My surgeon, Dr. Merrick Ross, at MD Anderson Cancer Center is wise, trustworthy, respected and a brilliant scientist and surgeon. What a blessing and God provision to have him as my doctor. He is kind, compassionate, and the very picture of excellence.

I was able to return home yesterday to heal and continue my ministry.

> O give thanks to the LORD, call on his name,
> make known his deeds among the peoples.
> Sing to him, sing praises to him,
> tell of all his wonderful works.
> Glory in his holy name;
> let the hearts of those who seek the Lord rejoice.
> Seek the LORD and his strength,
> seek his presence continually.
> —1Chronicles 16:8–11

Karen Kay Dunn and her family were living a somewhat predictable life. They would plan future events with confidence and those events would usually occur as planned. Two words changed that and shook the very foundation of this family. Those words were "invasive melanoma".

With the diagnosis of a cancer that is often referred to as, "the deadly skin cancer," nothing could be planned with confidence that it would be able to take place as scheduled in the future. In fact, no future was assured for Karen. Karen and her family were experiencing something very different. They now found themselves adjusting to living with uncertainty, because they no longer knew what their future would look like.

There are so many life situations that result in people needing to adjust themselves to living with uncertainty. Coping with loss, Alzheimer's, Parkinson's, cancer, accidents with permanent injuries, death, alienation from loved ones, financial ruin, and other trauma in life are some of those circumstances, but there are many more.

Living with uncertainty and still finding ways to enjoy life is an attainable goal! This book will familiarize you with some useful tools to bring peace and joy back despite enduring uninvited life circumstances. In this book, the reader is encouraged to overcome the devastating effects of a very painful life event by discovering a plan to accomplish that. It is helpful to both the person passing through the life crisis as well as family members and friends who are helping others in crisis.

As a mental health therapist, Who's Who in America Karen Kay Dunn has dedicated her life to helping people successfully walk through traumatic life events. She carefully presents a lifeline to readers who are dealing with life crises.

28834290R00117

Made in the USA
Columbia, SC
17 October 2018